For Pascale

Special thanks to the following contributors:

David Cooke
Lance Jensen

Their assistance was greatly appreciated.

D1614096

Contents

Introduction

Welcome Sun users. This guide will be your key to understanding your Sun workstation. Within these pages you will find out how to use all of the basic functions and capabilities in a minimal amount of time. From SunView to Security, from Backups to Permissions, you will find out what you need quickly.

This book is not intended to replace the current Sun documentation. It is a fast learning tool for you to become a functional Sun user quickly. Each chapter will cover the basic information needed to allow you to use that area efficiently. The chapters on UNIX file systems and permissions are for beginners' reference and will aid in learning the file system.

All examples will refer to the machine name `ltahoe`. This is done to make the references to a system prompt consistent and avoid confusion.

You should use this book in conjunction with the Sun manual pages included with your system. When referencing system commands or functions, the manual pages will give you the additional capabilities which will prove invaluable in the future.

I hope you enjoy this book and your new Sun workstation.

Note: At the time of publishing, there is a debate as to Sun Microsystems ownership of the term "Yellow Pages" which is described in chapter 10. Therefore all references to Yellow Pages in this book will be stated as "YP".

Logging into Your Sun System

Now that you have your system I'm sure you are ready to try it out. There are a few things you should know about it before you begin. You should have already been assigned or asked what you would like your account name to be by your system administrator. This will be your login name when you sign on to the system. You should have also been assigned a temporary password. This you can change once you have logged in.

After your system has been powered on you will see a login prompt with the system name followed by a login prompt.

```
ltahoe login:
```

1-1 Login Name

Here is where you will enter your login name. Once you have entered your login name you will be asked for a password.

```
ltahoe login: miker
password:
```

Enter your password now.

The system will not display the password as you type it. This is so nobody can peek over your shoulder while you enter your password. It is a simple, but important security feature.

If you do not have a password assigned to you, the system will not ask for a password. You should install a password immediately after you log in.

Note: Watch out for the caps lock key! There have been many users who claim that their password does not work when in fact they had accidentally bumped the caps lock key and were typing in capital letters.

Let's take a closer look at what actually happens when you log into your Sun workstation.

1-2 Password Entry

When you first enter your username at the login prompt, the system looks in the */etc/passwd* file to see if you are a valid user or not. This file is where the system keeps all entries of valid users and their passwords. A typical user entry in the password file will look like this:

miker:Hly45Ed0nF:3801:30:Michael Russo:/home/ltahoe/miker:/bin/csh

If you break down each field, you can see what the system is actually looking at.

miker	This is the username of the user. This would be you.
Hly45Ed0nF	This is the encrypted password. The system automaticaly encrypts the password. This is done when you first select a new password or change an existing one.
3801	This is the user's id number. It is unique for each user.
30	This is your group id number.
Michael Russo	User's real name. This is also how your name will appear as the sender in the header information in electronic mail. Mail is described in Chapter 9.
/home/ltahoe/miker	Users home directory location.
/bin/csh	The type of shell the user will use. This could be the C-Shell (csh), the Bourne Shell (sh), the Korn Shell (ksh), or it could even be noshell depending on the user type. The shell is the type of command interpreter that you will use. The shell reads commands from the command line and executes them. Different types of shells, like csh or sh, interpret special options differently. As far as UNIX commands go, they will all appear the same.

The system will read the */etc/passwd* file, verify your password, then start the login shell that is specified. Once the shell is started, the system will go to your home directory and look for your .cshrc and .login file. There it will read these files and set up your login session. (These files are defined in the section on your home directory).

1-3 Incorrect Login

If you mistype your login or password, the system will respond with "`login incorrect`" and will return you to the login prompt.

```
ltahoe login: mker
password:
login incorrect.
login:
```

Once you have logged in correctly, the system will display the "message of the day". This is a message that is kept in *letc/motd*. You can edit this file to say anything you like. It is a good idea to leave the original line in since it informs you of the operating system your machine is running.

You should now have your login prompt. An example login prompt will look like this:

```
ltahoe%
```

You may have a $ instead of a %. This would be the prompt for the Bourne Shell rather than the C-Shell.

Now that you have a login prompt you should change your password. This will ensure that you are the only one who can access your account. You should change your password at least once every two months for security reasons. When choosing a password, find a word you can remember easily. You can mix upper and lower case letters as well as including numbers. Do not use names of people as these are the easiest passwords to break. (See the section on security for password examples.)

1-4 Changing Your Password
Using the passwd Command

The **passwd** command allows you to change or install a password. The password can be for yourself or for the superuser referred to as "root". See Section 1-7 for information on superuser). The superuser is able to change the password for any user on the system. You must be the superuser (root), in order to change the password for root.

The basic syntax for the **passwd** command is:

```
ltahoe% passwd
```

The system will respond with:

```
ltahoe% changing password for (username) on
(systemname) old passwd:
```

You must enter the old password if you are changing an existing password. If you are installing your password for the first time, the system will ask you for "`new passwd:`"
(The system will not display your password as you type it.) You can now enter the new password. Once you have entered the new password the system will ask you to type in the password again. This will protect you from accidentally mis-typing in the wrong password and not knowing what it was that you typed in.

Once you have entered your password the second time, you will get your prompt back. If you wish you can test out your new password by logging out and back in again.

1-5 Changing Your YP Password

If you are running "yellow pages" (refered to as yp; see Section 10-3 for information on yp) and wish to change your "yp" password, you will need to use the yppasswd command. To change your yppassword, enter the command:

```
ltahoe% yppasswd
```

Change the password in the same manner as you did for your local password.

1-6 Logging Out

When you are not using your system you should either log out of the system, or bring up the lockscreen from SunView. There are several ways to log off of the system.
Use the **logout** command:

```
ltahoe% logout
ltahoe login:
```

You can use the exit command:

```
ltahoe% exit
ltahoe login:
```

Or you can log off with control-D. This is accomplished by holding down the control key and then pressing the "d" key. Although the "d" is shown as a capital letter, you do not need to use the shift key.

```
ltahoe% ^D
ltahoe login:
```

Note: If you have the "ignoreeof" variable set in your .login file, the control-D operation will not log you out. This variable prevents logout with control-D. (See the section on your home directory for details on ignoreeof.)

1-7 Logging in as "root" (Superuser)

There is a special user on your system. This is known as the "superuser" or "root". The superuser handles the administrative duties and has virtually unlimited access to all files on the system. Many commands can only be run as the superuser.

You must be extremely careful when doing work as root. You can cause severe problems on your system if you accidentally erase files that the system requires. The login to become the superuser is "**root**", followed by the password for root.

```
login: root
password:
ltahoe#
```

If your company allows the users root access, you should be sure you have a root password installed. If you do not, generate one by becoming the superuser and executing the **passwd** command just as you did for yourself. To become root after you have already logged into the system, simply enter the command: **su**

```
ltahoe% su
password:
ltahoe#
```

The "**su**" command stands for Substitute User; without a user name after it, "the command assumes" root as the substitute user. Notice the prompt is now a # sign. This is the superuser prompt. If

root did not have a password, you would not have been asked to
enter a password.

To leave superuser, simply type "**exit**"

```
ltahoe# exit
ltahoe%
```

Check with your system administrator to find out what access you
are allowed as root. If you have superuser privileges on your system, you must take care in protecting the password so that nobody
else can find out what it is. Please be careful with root privileges as
it is very powerful and if you are on a network of systems, you could
cause a great deal of damage.

Basic File System

2

2-1 Understanding the File System

In order to use your Sun system correctly you must first understand the way UNIX file systems are structured. If you already have an understanding of UNIX files and file systems, you may want to skim over this section as a refresher, just in case.

If you are a beginning UNIX user or have not yet fully understood how file systems really work, then let's get this mystery solved and make you a functional UNIX user.

For as long as can be remembered, anyone who has tried to explain what a file system is, always references a file cabinet as the parent directory, with its drawers as sub-directories, and the files in the directories as the actual paper files in the drawer.

This seems obscure, but it must hold true because everyone seems to use it. So let's start by describing the basic file system as it is used on your system.

All file systems start with a parent directory. This is the initial directory in which all other directories exist. You call this directory "/" or the root directory. Under this directory will be all of the sub-directories and files.

If you look at the components of a file system, they would consist of the following:

Directory   An area which holds files and other directories (called sub-directories).
File   A folder which holds data.

A directory can contain any number of sub-directories. These sub-directories can contain more sub-directories as well as files. This can go on and on and on. You can move through these directories and look at what is contained within them.

In order to move through the file system you must specify a path to the next directory. This is referred to as the pathname. Think of the pathname as giving the system a route to a file or directory. This can be like telling a friend how to get to your house.

Your friend will need to know the names of the streets, just as the system will need to know the names of the directories to pass through.

The routes between directories are separated with a / (slash). So the pathname to a chess program on the system could be: */home/miker/games/chess*

Path to a chess program.

Starting from / , the path would be /home/miker/games/chess

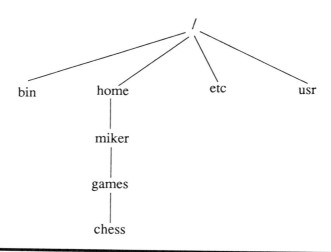

FIGURE 2.1. *Following the path from the root directory to a chess program.*

Notice that the directory names are separated with a /. The slash symbol really has two meanings:

1. To separate routes between directories.
2. As a symbol for the root directory.

2-2 Basic File System Commands

You should first look at a few commands that will help you look and travel through the file system. The basic commands for this are the following:

cd   Change directory
           Use: `ltahoe%` *cd (pathname)*
           This command allows you to move around in the file system.
           The cd command without a pathname will move you into your
           home directory.

ls   List
           Use: `ltahoe%` ls -(**options**) *(directoryname)*
           This will allow you to list the contents
           of a directory.

pwd   Print working directory
           Use: `ltahoe%` **pwd**
           This command will display the current
           working directory.

The ls command will list the contents of a directory. It will display these contents in alphabetical order and arrange them into columns. Try listing the contents of the "/" or root directory.

    `ltahoe%` **ls** /

```
shelltool - /bin/csh
ltahoe% ls /
bin               export          lost+found       tmp
boot              home            mnt              usr
dev               kadb            sbin             var
etc               lib             sys              vmunix
ltahoe%
```

FIGURE 2.2. *Output of the ls command.*

This output of ls shows the names of the files and directories but will not tell you which is which. One way to see which of the names in your listing are files and which are directories, is to use the -F option to the ls command. This will append a "/" after each directory name, a "*" after each file, and a "@" for a symbolic link (a pointer to another file). Here is the same listing for the root directory but with the -F option.

But what if you wanted to see more information about your

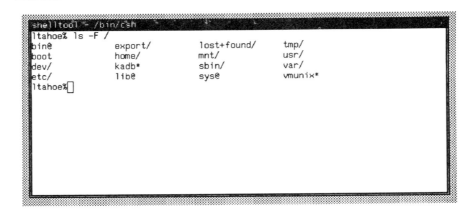

```
shelltool - /bin/csh
ltahoe% ls -F /
bin@            export/         lost+found/     tmp/
boot            home/           mnt/            usr/
dev/            kadb*           sbin/           var/
etc/            lib@            sys@            vmunix*
ltahoe%
```

FIGURE 2.3. *Output of ls with -F option.*

directory? What if you wanted to know who owns the files and directories? For this you will use the -l option to the ls command. The -l option will produce an output that will tell you most everything about the files and directories. Try the -l option to ls on the root file system.

    ltahoe% ls -l /

Now you have much more information about your root file

```
shelltool - /bin/csh
ltahoe% ls -l /
total 1484
lrwxrwxrwx   1 root             7 Jan  5 15:54 bin -> usr/bin
-r--r--r--   1 root        110912 Jan  5 16:45 boot
drwxr-sr-x   2 bin           7680 Jan  8 13:35 dev
drwxr-sr-x   7 bin           1536 Jan 10 07:49 etc
drwxr-sr-x   4 root           512 Jan  5 15:54 export
drwxr-xr-x   5 root           512 Jan  5 17:00 home
-rwxr-xr-x   1 root        239783 Jan  5 16:45 kadb
lrwxrwxrwx   1 root             7 Jan  5 15:54 lib -> usr/lib
drwxr-xr-x   2 root          8192 Jan  5 15:51 lost+found
drwxr-sr-x   2 bin           512 Nov  6 18:05 mnt
drwxr-sr-x   2 bin           512 Jan  5 16:45 sbin
lrwxrwxrwx   1 root            13 Jan  5 15:54 sys -> ./usr/kvm/sys
drwxrwsrwt   2 bin           512 Jan 10 15:11 tmp
drwxr-xr-x  21 root           512 Jan 10 14:22 usr
drwxr-xr-x  11 root           512 Nov  6 18:28 var
-rwxr-xr-x   1 root       1101191 Jan  8 07:41 vmunix
ltahoe%
```

FIGURE 2.4. *Listing of / or (root) filesystem.*

system. If you look at the first character for each listing you will see either an l,-,or d. The "l" stands for a link to another file or directory. This means that the data does not reside under this directory but the link shows you where the actual data resides. If there is a "-" for the first character it will be a file. The "d" stands for a directory of which there can be sub-directories and files underneath it. Do not worry about the rest of the information that is supplied with the -l option for now, you will look at this a little later.

If you wanted to look at the contents of the directory called *usr*, you would specify the path to usr from the root directory. Since / is the root directory, you would give the following path to the ls command:

    ltahoe% ls -l /usr

```
shelltool - /bin/csh
ltahoe%ls -l /usr
total 51
drwxr-sr-x   2 bin          512 Nov  6 20:28 5lib
lrwxrwxrwx   1 root          10 Jan  5 16:16 adm -> ../var/adm
drwxr-sr-x   3 bin         4608 Jan  5 16:33 bin
lrwxrwxrwx   1 root          10 Jan  5 16:15 boot -> ./kvm/boot
drwxr-sr-x  13 bin          512 Jan  5 16:44 demo
drwxr-sr-x   2 bin          512 Nov  6 19:40 diag
drwxr-sr-x   3 bin          512 Nov  6 19:10 dict
drwxrwxr-x   8 root         512 Nov 17 11:14 doctools
drwxr-sr-x   5 bin         3072 Jan  5 16:33 etc
drwxr-sr-x   2 bin          512 Jan  5 15:54 export
drwxr-sr-x   5 root        1536 Nov 10 18:14 games
drwxr-sr-x   2 bin          512 Nov  6 19:16 hosts
drwxr-sr-x  41 bin         2048 Jan  5 16:27 include
drwxr-sr-x   6 root        1024 Jan  5 16:20 kvm
drwxr-sr-x  18 bin         2560 Jan  5 16:33 lib
drwxrwsr-x  28 root         512 Jan  3 21:35 local
drwxr-xr-x   2 root        8192 Jan  5 15:53 lost+found
lrwxrwxrwx   1 root           9 Jan  5 16:16 man -> share/man
lrwxrwxrwx   1 root          10 Jan  5 16:16 mdec -> ./kvm/mdec
lrwxrwxrwx   1 root           8 Jan  5 16:27 net -> /var/net
lrwxrwxrwx   1 root          13 Jan  5 16:27 nserve -> ../etc/nserve
drwxr-sr-x   2 bin         1024 Jan  5 16:31 old
lrwxrwxrwx   1 root          13 Jan  5 16:16 pub -> share/lib/pub
drwxr-sr-x   3 bin          512 Nov  6 19:23 sccs
drwxr-sr-x   5 bin          512 Nov  6 19:48 share
lrwxrwxrwx   1 root          12 Jan  5 16:16 spool -> ../var/spool
lrwxrwxrwx   1 root           9 Jan  5 16:16 src -> share/src
lrwxrwxrwx   1 root          11 Jan  5 16:16 stand -> ./kvm/stand
lrwxrwxrwx   1 root           7 Jan  5 16:16 sys -> kvm/sys
lrwxrwxrwx   1 root          10 Jan  5 16:16 tmp -> ../var/tmp
drwxr-sr-x   2 bin         1536 Jan  5 16:33 ucb
lrwxrwxrwx   1 root           9 Jan  5 16:16 ucbinclude -> ./include
lrwxrwxrwx   1 root           3 Jan  5 16:16 ucblib -> lib
ltahoe%
```

FIGURE 2.5. *Listing of /usr filesystem.*

As you can see there are more directories under this one.

Now let's look at the contents of the directory under /usr called games. All you have to do is specify the path to the directory you want to look at. Remember all directories in the path are separated with a / .

    ltahoe% ls -l /usr/games

```
shelltool - /bin/csh
ltahoe% ls /usr/games
adventure      canfieldtool    fortune       moria        robots
arithmetic     cfscores        gammonscore   mpss         snake
asteroids      chess           gammontool    nlock        snscore
backgammon     chesstool       hack          number       stocktool
bandit         ching           hangman       ogre         suntetris
banner         conquer         hunt          omega        suntetris.hs
battlestar     craps           lib           palettetool  teachgammon
bcd            cribbage        life          paranoia     tetra
bj             crumble         mahjongg      primes       trek
bogdict        dclock          man           qix          wanderer
boggle         doc             maze          qt           world
boggledict     eyecon          mazewar       quiz         worm
boggletool     faces           mille         rain         worms
btlgammon      factor          monop         rainbow      wump
canfield       fish            moo           random
ltahoe%
```

FIGURE 2.6. *Listing of /usr/games directory.*

2-3 Creating Files

You have seen directories, but what about files? Files can be anything from a list of phone numbers, a recipe for meatloaf, or a program to calculate the origin of life. All that is required of a file is that it have a name tied to the data. Let's create a file in your home directory and call it numbers. First you must change directories into your home directory. To do this simply enter the cd command at your prompt and hit return. Then verify that you are in your own directory by using the pwd command.

```
ltahoe% cd
ltahoe% pwd
/home/ltahoe/miker
```

Touch

To create an empty file, you can use the **touch** command. This will create a blank file with the name you specify. To use the **touch** command simply enter:

```
ltahoe% touch numbers
```

Now if you execute the **ls** command in your directory, you will see the file numbers.

```
ltahoe% ls
numbers
```

By using **vi** (visual editor) or some other editor, you can input data into the file. (See the chapter on editors for information about vi.)

2-4 Removing Files

To remove a file you do not want anymore, you will use the "**rm**" command. To use the **rm** command, enter at the system prompt: **rm** (filename)

```
ltahoe% rm (filename)
```

Note: Be sure you want to remove a file before you use the **rm** command. Once removed, it is gone for good. You can use the -i option to the **rm** command to help protect yourself against accidental erasures. This will make the system ask you if you are sure you want to remove a file before it does the actual removal. In the section on your home directory, you will set the -i option to **rm** as an alias. This means that you will always be asked to verify that you wish to remove the file.

2-5 Viewing Files

When you create files, you are sure to want to review them in the future. To bring up the contents of a file you can use the following commands.

cat   This command will display a named file to the screen. If the
         file is longer that one screenful, you will only see the last
         page of the file as the rest would have already scrolled
         past you.

more   This will display the file in the same manner as the **cat**
         command, but will display only one screenful at a time.

view   This will display the contents of the file but in a vi format. This
         way you can scroll around and search for strings within the file.
         You cannot write to the file with view.

The Cat and More Command

Each command is entered at the system prompt followed by the
filename you wish to see. If you wish to see a file that is not in the
current directory, you must specify the path to that file.

The **cat** command will work fine for small files but for longer
ones, the **more** command is preferred. Using **more** allows you
to see the entire file a windowful at a time. When using the
more command on a long file, the screen will fill up with the contents of the file and a highlighted box will appear at the bottom
with the word "more" and a percentage of the file you have
seen so far. To see the rest of the file, use the space bar to
move ahead one screenful at a time, or the return key, to move
ahead one line at a time. To exit the **more** command, simple
enter a "q". This will stop the output and return you to the
prompt.

Here is what the **more** command will output on a file in etc
called ttytab. (See Figure 2.7.)

    ltahoe% more /etc/ttytab

View

The "**view**" command works just like **vi** except that you cannot
write to the file. In this way you can use all of the vi features to
move around and search in a file. (See Figure 2.8.)

    ltahoe% view /etc/ttytab

After you have created a few files of your own, try each of the
commands.

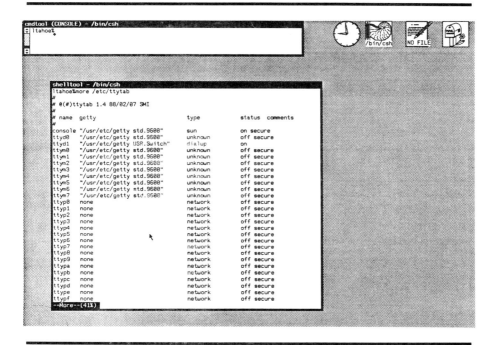

FIGURE 2.7. *Output of the more command on the /etc/ttytab File.*

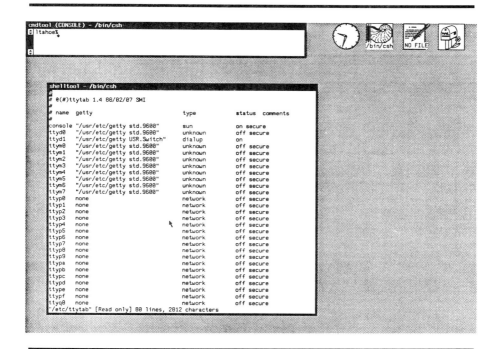

FIGURE 2.8. *Output of view command on /etc/ttytab File.*

2-6 Special Files

There are special files that begin with a period and are called dot files. They do not appear on the screen when you use the **ls** command. These are your environment files like *.login* and *.cshrc*. Since these files rarely change, it is not necessary to see them when you look at the contents of your home directory. If you wish to see all files in a directory including the .files, you will need to use the -a option to the **ls** command. When you use the **ls -al** command you will see two directories called "." and "..". The "." shows the permissions on the directory of which the **ls -la** command was performed. The ".." shows the permissions on the parent directory of that directory. You can also use the . and .. with the cd command. If you wanted to use cd to go up one level in the directory path, you would enter:

```
ltahoe% cd ..
```

Now you would be in the next directory level up in the path.

```
ltahoe% pwd
/home/games
ltahoe% cd ..
ltahoe% pw
 /home
ltahoe%
```

2-7 Creating Directories

To create a new directory under your home directory, you will use the **mkdir** command. This command will make a new directory with the name you specify. To use the **mkdir** command, simply enter from your prompt:

```
ltahoe% mkdir (directory name)
```

Note: You can only create a new directory under one in which you have write permission. (See the section on permissions.)

Create a directory called *"mystuff"* under your home directory.

```
ltahoe% mkdir mystuff
ltahoe% ls
mystuff  numbers
```

Now you can use **cd** to get into the directory *mystuff* and create more directories or files.

You should never have a flat file system. A flat file system occurs when you save all of your files in your home directory, rather than creating specific directories under your home directory and placing your files within them.

You should create a directory for files like *mail, phonenumb, status-reports, daily-tasks*, etc. Then place any files which match the category under the appropriate directory. If you do not have a directory which matches the file subject, make one. This way when looking for a file, you will have only a few directories to search through, rather than hundreds of files.

2-8 Removing Directories

To remove a directory, use the **rmdir** command. You need to be one directory level higher than the directory you wish to remove. In other words, you cannot be inside the directory you are removing. If there are files located in the directory you wish to remove, you can use the **rm** command with the -r option.

```
ltahoe% rmdir (directoryname)
```

2-9 Understanding the ls Command

Previously you looked at a listing of some directories with the -l option to **ls.** This listing contained lots of information about the files and directories contained within. Let's see what all that information means.

If you executed the **ls -l** command on the root filesystem, you would get an output that looks like this:

```
ltahoe% ls -l /
```

```
shelltool - /bin/csh
ltahoe% ls -l /
total 1484
lrwxrwxrwx   1 root            7 Jan  5 15:54 bin -> usr/bin
-r--r--r--   1 root       110912 Jan  5 16:45 boot
drwxr-sr-x   2 bin          7680 Jan  8 13:35 dev
drwxr-sr-x   7 bin          1536 Jan 10 07:49 etc
drwxr-sr-x   4 root          512 Jan  5 15:54 export
drwxr-xr-x   5 root          512 Jan  5 17:00 home
-rwxr-xr-x   1 root       239783 Jan  5 16:45 kadb
lrwxrwxrwx   1 root            7 Jan  5 15:54 lib -> usr/lib
drwxr-xr-x   2 root         8192 Jan  5 15:51 lost+found
drwxr-sr-x   2 bin           512 Nov  6 18:05 mnt
drwxr-sr-x   2 bin           512 Jan  5 16:45 sbin
lrwxrwxrwx   1 root           13 Jan  5 15:54 sys -> ./usr/kvm/sys
drwxrwsrwt   2 bin           512 Jan 10 14:11 tmp
drwxr-xr-x  20 root          512 Jan  5 16:27 usr
drwxr-xr-x  11 root          512 Nov  6 18:28 var
-rwxr-xr-x   1 root      1101191 Jan  8 07:41 vmunix
ltahoe%
```

FIGURE 2.9. *Output of ls -l Command on / or (root) filesystem.*

Now let's look at all of the fields in order and see what they represent. Here is a chart to show you each field.

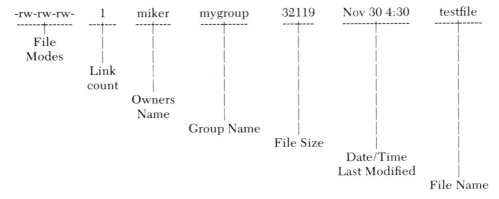

File Modes: This field tells you what the current permissions are for this file or directory. For a detailed definition of file modes, see the chapter on permissions.

Link Count: For directories, it tells you the number of sub-directories under it. For files it is usually a 1.

Owner Name: This is the owner of the file or directory.

Group Name: This is the group name that the owner of the file belonged to when he created the file. NOTE: This is only displayed with the -g option to the ls command.

File Size: This is the size of the file in bytes. If it were a text file, it would show the number of characters in the file.

Modification Time: This shows the last time the file or directory was modified. If you look at the listing of /, you can see that some directories have dates with times, while some have dates with the year. This happens when a file has not been modified for over one year.

File Name: This is the actual name of the file or directory.
    As you can see the -l option gives you a lot of information about files and directories. It is the option you will use the most when looking at files. Here are a few other options to the ls command that you will find useful.
    Note: Some options to the ls command require the -l option first. That is, certain options must have a long listing to support that particular options function.

-a   list all files inlcuding "." files.
-d   This will allow you to look at just a directory itself without
        looking at the contents of the directory. Used with the -l option.
-g   This will show you the group name when used with the -l option.

2-10 Moving and Renaming Files

There are instances where you may need to move a file or directory from one location to another. This is accomplished with the "**mv**" command. To move a file from one directory to the next, simply enter the name of the file you wish to move and the directory you wish to move it to. You may also rename a file to another name. Let's start by moving a file in */home* called *memos*, to a directory called */home/junk/memos*. The command for this would be:

```
ltahoe% mv   /home/memos   /home/junk/memos.
```

The junk directory under */home* must already exist before the move will work.

Rename

You can rename a file with the mv command by specifying the new name after the old name. Here is an example of renaming a file:

```
ltahoe% mv memos letters
```

If you were to list the contents of the directory where *memos* was located, there would now be a letters file in its place.

You can also rename a file with the copy command (**cp**). This will give you the new filename and still keep the old file. This is also safer than move because you will still have the original file.

```
ltahoe% cp memos letters
```

You would now have a file called *memos* and a file called *letters*. Both are the same file, just different names.

The only way to get good at something is to practice. Play around in your home directory with the commands you have seen. Look at the man pages for more information about the commands. (refer to the section on manpages) Play until you feel comfortable with each area of the file system.

File Permissions

3-1 Basic File Permissions

In this section you will look at what file permission and ownership means and what you will need to know to understand how they work.

The UNIX system provides a method in which to assign permissions to files and directories so that the types of users who can access the files can be controlled.

All of the files and directories which are created on the system have an owner. This is usually the user who created the file originally. This owner has the capability to assign permissions to the file so that only certain users may gain access to the file.

For all files and directories there are three classes of users who you can assign access to.

OWNER: The owner is the person who originally created the file or directory. The owner can change the ownership to someone else by using the "chown" command. (See the chown command later in this section.)

GROUP: You can have several users isolated in a group which can have access to your files. This relates to the group id number in your password file entry.

OTHER: This category means anyone who can get to your files may access them. This category is sometimes referred to as "world" or "public".

Each category (owner, group, other) has three types of permissions associated with them. These permissions are the types of things you can do with a directory or file. The three types of permissions are:

READ (r)   WRITE (w)   EXECUTE (x)

READ: A user who has read permission to a file may look at the contents of that file. A user who has read permission to a directory may look at the files contained within that directory.

WRITE: A user who has write permissions to a file may change the contents of that file. A user who has write permission to a directory may remove or add new files.

EXECUTE: This means that a user can execute that file as a command. Directories need execute (x) permissions in order to cd into the directory and also read (r) permission to copy files into the directory.

If you took all three categories and placed them together, you would see them side by side and they would appear as nine separate permissions, each controlling its separate category. The display of the permissions looks like this:

    rwxrwxrwx

If you break down this line into the separate categories it would appear as:

r w x	r w x	r w x
- - -	- - -	- - -
owner	group	other

You can display the permissions of any file by using the -l option to the ls command.

If you perform an ls -l of a directory called /home/ltahoe

    ltahoe% ls -l **/home/ltahoe**

the output looks like this:

    drwxrwxr-x 5 root   1024 Oct 1 18:52 ltahoe

If you look at the first character of the permissions field, there is a "d". This means that you are looking at a directory. If this were a file, there would have been a "-" in place of the d.

Let's examine the permissions on */home/ltahoe*. If you break down the permissions you will see the following:

- The owner (root) has read, write, and execute permission

- The group has read, write, and execute permission

- All others have only read and execute permission.

If there is a "-" in place of a permission, this means that the class of user does not have that permission. So in this case, "others" do not have write permission to this directory.

There are certain types of permissions you will want on specific files and directories. For example, files located within your home directory you would probably not want just anyone to look at (like your resume). On these files you will want the permissions to be set so that only you can read or write the file. Let's say there is a resume file in your home directory. The permissions you would want to have would be:

-rw-------

This would give only the owner (you) the right to look at or alter this file.

3-2 Using **chmod**

When you look at the permissions of a file or directory, you are said to be looking at it's "mode". The mode of a file or directory may be changed with a command called "**chmod**". The "chmod" command will allow you (the owner) or the superuser to alter the permissions of a file or directory.

The basic syntax of the "**chmod**" command is:

`ltahoe% chmod [mode] filename`

where mode is the value of the new mode.

Do you remember earlier when you looked at the three fields of users? Each field had three sets of permissions---

rwx   rwx   rwx

What you want to do is translate the fields into an octal format. If you do not know or care what an octal representation is then you can look at it this way. Let's assign a number to each fields permission.

Own	Grp	Oth
421	421	421
rwx	rwx	rwx

If you were to add up each fields permissions as a number, it would be:

```
owner  4+2+1=7
group  4+2+1=7
other  4+2+1=7
```

So in this example, the mode is 777 which relates to rwxrwxrwx or all permissions set on.

Now let's change the mode so that the owner can read, write

and execute, the group can read and execute and the others can only read.

The permissions of such a file would be rwxr-xr-- Change it to an octal value.

```
421     421     421
rwx     r-x     r--
```

If you add up all the permissions that are "on", you would have a resulting mode of:

```
              r  w  x
owner      4+2+1= 7
              r  w
group      4+1    = 5
              r
other      4      = 4
                 or..754
```

So the command to make this change would look like:

ltahoe% **chmod 754 filename**

The permissions on this file would now look like this:

-rwxr-xr--

Try a practical example. Use cd to get into the directory called /tmp and create a file called *"perm"*.

ltahoe% **cd /tmp**
ltahoe% **touch perm**   (Remember the **touch** command creates an
                            empty file.)

If you do an ls -l of the file perm

ltahoe% **ls -l perm**
-rw-r--r-- 1 miker   0 Oct 28 11:49 perm

Change the permission of the file *"perm"* so that the categories "group" and "other" can have write permission to the file.

ltahoe% **chmod 766 perm**
ltahoe% **ls-l perm**
-rwxrw-rw- 1 miker   0 Oct 28 11:49 perm

Now anyone may write to the file *perm*.

There is also a symbolic method to change the permissions to a file or directory. This may seem confusing to the beginning UNIX user, but a brief explanation is only fair.

You can change the permission to the file you created in /tmp using character representations of the modes you wish.

Here is a list of the character abbreviations for the different categories, operations and permissions.

category:

u	owner permissions
g	group permissions
o	other permissions
a	all categories of permissions

operation:

=	add this permission explicitly, remove the rest
+	add a permission
−	subtract this permission

permissions:

r	Read.
w	Write.
x	Execute.
X	Give execute permission if the file is a directory or if there is execute permission for one of the other user classes.
s	Set owner- or group-ID. This is only useful with u or g. Also, the set group-ID bit of a directory may only be modified with + or −. You will see more about the "s" permission below.
t	Set the sticky bit. This will keep the program in memory to save time when executing.

Try to change the permissions of the file perm so that the group has execute (x) permission to the file. The basic syntax for using character representation is:

%chmod {u,g,o,a} {+,−,+} {r,w,x,X,s,t}

To change the file so the group has permission:

```
ltahoe% chmod g+x perm
ltahoe% ls -l perm
-rwxrwxrw- 1 miker    0 Oct 28 11:49 perm
```

Now the group category has execute permission on the file.

You may also combine the commands so as to make more than one change to the permissions. For instance;

```
ltahoe% chmod go+w perm
```

This will change the file so that the "group" and "other" categories have write permissions.

Try changing the file to other modes to test your prowess.

There are many combinations of the **chmod** command. Take a peek at the man page on chmod for more detailed explanations.

3-3 Changing the Ownership with **chown**

The chown command will change the ownership of a file from the current owner to another user. If you create a directory under */home* called *genesis,* and you create this directory as root, the owner of the directory will be root. If you want the user pascale to own this directory, you will need to change the ownership of the directory to pascale. Since you were root when you created the directory, you need to be root to change the ownership.

```
ltahoe# mkdir /home/genesis
ltahoe# ls -l /home
drwxr-xr-x 2 root    512 Jan 31 20:03    genesis
ltahoe# chown pascale genesis
ltahoe# ls -l /home
drwxr-xr-x 2 pascale    512 Jan 31 20:03    genesis
ltahoe#
```

You must either own the file or directory, or be root in order to change the ownership.

3-4 Setting the "group-id" and "user-id"

Setting the group-id and user-id allows others to have the same permissions as the file or directory have when executing them. The permission is displayed with the "s" permisson when the -l option is used in with the **ls** command.

A good example of the set user-id bit is with the **passwd** command. This command allows you to edit the password file to change your user password. The password file is owned by root and can only be written to by root. Yet you can change your own password with the **passwd** command. So how is this done? If you look at the permissions on the */etc/passwd* file, they will appear as:

```
ltahoe% ls -l /etc/passwd
-rw-r--r-- 1 root    402 Nov 11 10:02    etcpasswd
```

As you can see anyone can read the file but only root can actually edit the file.

Now let's look at the permissions on the **passwd** command itself:

```
ltahoe% ls -l /bin/passwd
-rwsr-xr-x 3 root      24576 Apr 9    /bin/passwd
```

Notice the first category of permissions is -rws. This means that whoever executes this command will have the same permissions as the owner of the command. In this case root is the owner. So that means that you have write permission to the */etc/passwd* file.

The group-id bit works the same way. If the group-id bit is set, then anyone who executes the command will have the same permissions as the group.

To set these permissions you will use the + or - options with the **chmod** command. So to change the permissions of your perm file so it has the user-id bit set, you would type the command:

```
ltahoe% chmod u+s perm
```

Now if you do an **ls -l** of perm:

```
ltahoe% ls -l perm
-rwsrw-rw- 1 miker      0 Nov 19 13:57 perm
```

If you notice the execute permission is covered up by the "s" permission, don't be alarmed. It is still there. But, if the "s" were a "S", then the execute permission would not have been allowed. So remember, if it is a capital S, then it is the same as if there is a - behind the S; if it is a lower case s, then the permission is active behind the s.

3-5 Setting the Default Permissions with **umask**

The default mode of newly created files and directories is controlled by the umask or "user mask". You may display the current umask value by entering the command "**umask**" without any options.

```
ltahoe% umask
002
ltahoe%
```

This would give a newly created file the mode of:

rw-rw-r--

Since the 2 would be the write permission for the category of other, it is masked out and is not allowed. Another way to see how this works would be if you subtracted the new default from the current default. Suppose your current default is 666 (rw-rw-rw) and you would like them to be 644 (rw-r--r--), then you could subtract the two modes and come up with the new umask.

```
 666
-644
 ----
 022
```

At this point you can set your new default value for your files by entering the command:

1tahoe% **umask 022**

Please remember that directories need to be executable and the umask will make all directories executable automatically.

If you change the current <u>unmask</u> during a login session and you log out without editing your *.login* file, the next time you log back in, the old <u>umask</u> will be in effect. If you wish to keep "your" <u>umask</u>, then you must enter this into your .login file. (You will find this under the chapter on your home directory.)

Manual Pages

4

4-1 Using On-Line Man Pages

The system has included with the Sun Operating System (SunOS) Release, a complete set of manual pages which you can access from your system. Typically they are NFS mounted from a file server somewhere, or they may reside on your own local disk. A description of NFS mounts are in the chapter on networking. These manual pages are a means to where you can reference information about a command on your system, without having to search through a thousand pages of reference manuals to find the information you need.

To access the manual pages, simply enter the command **man** followed by the name of the command you wish to see the documentation on. The man pages can be accessed anywhere you may be in the file system.
Example:

```
ltahoe% man cd
```

The system will then print the manual page for the **cd** command. (This is a small man page, it is intended only as an example.) (See Figure 4.1.)

Here is the information that the man page will give you. It will vary depending on the command. Some commands may have twenty pages of text, while others will have only one. When there is more than one page of text, man will display the output through the **more** command. To display the next page of text, hit the space bar. To move one line at a time, hit the return key.

Name	The name and purpose of the command.
Synopsis	How to use the command.
Description	A description of what the command does.
Options	A list of options to the command, listed in alphabetical order along with a description of each option.

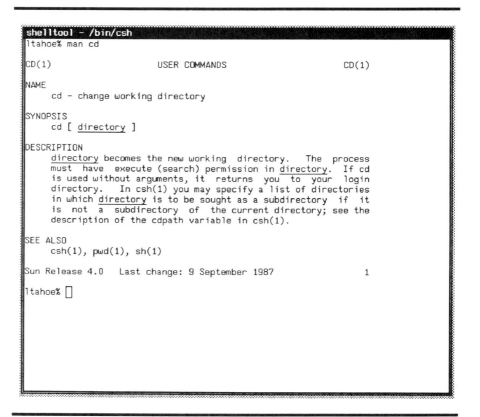

```
shelltool - /bin/csh
ltahoe% man cd

CD(1)                          USER COMMANDS                          CD(1)

NAME
      cd - change working directory

SYNOPSIS
      cd [ directory ]

DESCRIPTION
      directory becomes the new working  directory.   The  process
      must  have  execute (search) permission in directory.  If cd
      is used without arguments, it  returns  you  to  your  login
      directory.   In csh(1) you may specify a list of directories
      in which directory is to be sought as a subdirectory  if  it
      is  not  a  subdirectory  of  the current directory; see the
      description of the cdpath variable in csh(1).

SEE ALSO
      csh(1), pwd(1), sh(1)

Sun Release 4.0   Last change: 9 September 1987                        1

ltahoe% []
```

FIGURE 4-1. *Output of the manual page on ls*

Commands	A list of commands that can be run in conjunction with the named command.
Files	A list of files that are associated with this command.
See Also	A list of information about other commands and documentation that will help you understand the named command.
Diagnostics	Will show you a list of diagnostic messages that you may encounter.
Bugs	A list of known bugs with this command.

You should look at the man page for each command you learn, if anything just to see what other options there are to the command. You will be surprised to find that many commands have several useful features you would not have normally known about.

-k Option

You can use the -k option to the **man** command to find a "keyword" if you are unsure of the actual command name. For instance, if you wanted to see any manpage that references a clock, you would enter the command:

```
ltahoe% man -k clock
adjtime (2) - correct the time to allow
synchronization of the system clock
clock (1) - display the time in an icon or
window
clock (3C) - report CPU time used
cron (8) - clock daemon
```

Notice there are several instances of "clock"; each is followed by the section of the manpage that it is located in. To look at the clock title which reports the cpu time, you would enter the command:

ltahoe% **man 3c clock**

This would display the Section 3c manpage for clock. If no specification for a specific title is given, then the system will display a command title before a function.

4-2 Setting the MANPATH Variable

There is a variable you can set called "MANPATH", which will tell the system where to look for other manual pages. Your system administrator may have installed optional manual pages on a file server. In your .cshrc file you can add the path to these optional manual pages by inserting the line:

setenv MANPATH pathname:pathname:pathname:etc

The pathname is the path to the directory which contains the manual pages. Multiple paths are separated with a ":". This option is described in the chapter on your home directory. It is here for your information and will be explained in detail in Chapter 7.

Executing Commands

5

5-1 Using Commands

When you execute commands on the system, you need to follow some basic rules so that the command can perform its task correctly. The basic rules for entering commands are that the command is the first word, followed by arguments to the command, separated by a space. There are several types of arguments to UNIX commands. They are:

Options	Options are entered after the command. They usually start with a "-". Options tell the command that you wish to perform special functions that the command has available to it. You need to look at the man page for the specified command to see what options are available. Most commands have many special options and they are different for each command.
Expressions	Expressions can be a word or string of words which act as input to a specific command. Only certain commands use expressions. The "**grep**" command for example, is one of these. **Grep** is a command which searches for character matches in a file. **Grep** is described further in Section 5-10.
Filename	This would be the name of the file or files you wish to perform the command on. The filename can be up to 14 characters in length and can also be specified by any of the special characters which can denote a filename. A "." for instance, represents the current working directory.

So the basic rule for commands are:

      command   option   expression   filename

The command is entered at the prompt, followed by a space, then any of the above parts that the command requires. All parts must be separated by a space, and terminated with a carriage return. When the command is completed, the system will return to the prompt.

Some commands do not have to have any arguments in order to function. Some examples of these commands are the **ls, date,** and **pwd** command. Although they have options available to them, it is not necessary to enter them. An example is the **date** command, which will simply give you the date when entered alone. If you wanted to change the date, then you would need to give the date command an argument to make the change.

5-2 Aborting Commands

There will be times when you will want to abort a command which you have started to execute. To do this, you need to enter a Ctrl C, (Control key, then the c key) while the command is trying to execute. It will appear on the screen as a ˆC.

Let's say you were using the grep command to search for a file in a large directory, then remembered where the file was that you were searching for (remember the grep command is used to search for characters in file or directory). You would terminate the grep command with a Ctrl C.

```
ltahoe% ls -R /home |grep lostfile
ˆC
ltahoe%
```

The grep command has now been aborted.

5-3 Suspending Commands

You have the ability to suspend, or temporarily stop a command. This is accomplished with a Ctrl Z. (Hold down the control key, then depress the z key). This key sequence will suspend the command until you are ready to re-activate it. To re-activate the command, enter "fg" which means "foreground". An example would be if you were in vi, editing a file, and wanted to stop the editing for a moment to look at some other data. You would enter the Ctrl Z sequence, which would suspend the vi session, and place you at the command prompt. Then you could look at the data you needed to see, then enter "fg" at the prompt. You would then be back in the vi session.

You have the ability to suspend more than one process at a time on your system. You can suspend and background jobs, then call them back with the "%" symbol followed by the background job number. To find the background job number, enter the command "jobs".

Try to suspend several vi jobs, then call them back. Via new
file named *test1*, now suspend the vi process with a Ctrl Z.
The system will respond with "Stopped", followed by the
prompt. Now enter **vi** again and edit a file called test2. Suspend
this one as well and repeat the process again for a file called test3.
You should now have three vi jobs running, all are suspended. To
look at the jobs which are suspended, enter the command:

```
ltahoe% jobs
1       Stopped     vi test1
2    -  Stopped     vi test2
3    +  Stopped     vi test3
ltahoe%
```

Now you can bring any one of the jobs to the foreground by using
the % symbol, followed by the job number. So, if you wanted to
restart the editing session on the file test2, you would enter the
command:

ltahoe% %2

You should now be in vi ready to edit the file *test2*. Notice the "-"
and "+" sign after the job number on the second and third jobs.
You could also bring either of these jobs to the foreground with a
"+" or a "-" after the "%" symbol. The "%" symbol followed by a
"+" sign would bring forward job 3, a "-" sign would bring forward
job 2.

5-4 Background Processing

You have just seen how to suspend a command. Now let's see
how you can put jobs in the background where they can run on
their own.

Since UNIX is a multi-tasking system, where you can run
many tasks at the same time, you will need to be able to start a task,
then have the system go off and complete it, while you continue on
with other tasks. Commands are completed when the prompt is
returned to the user. But what if you need the prompt back while
the fist task is executing? Here is where backgrounding comes in.
Let's say you want to play a game of chess. If you start the **chess**
command, the prompt will not return until you complete or abort
the game. You can start the game in the background, and the
system will keep the game running, yet you will have your prompt
back, ready to do other things.

To start a process running in the background, add a "**&**" symbol to the end of the command.

```
ltahoe% chess &
1 255
ltahoe%
```

The system displayed the job number along with the system process number, then gave you the prompt back. The chess game is now running, and you can continue to enter commands at the prompt.

Let's try another example. While in SunView, start up another shelltool from an existing shelltool.

```
ltahoe% shelltool
```

You will not get the prompt back because the current shell is being used to run the other shelltool in the foreground. Quit the shelltool and try this example again, only this time add the "**&**" symbol after the shelltool command.

```
ltahoe% shelltool &
ltahoe%
```

The new shelltool is running in the background and you can continue to use the existing shelltool for other uses.

You can also background a process you have already started. To do this you will need to suspend the process with the Ctrl Z sequence, then enter "**bg**" (background). This will take the suspended process and restart it, only now it will be running in the background.

Try this example. Start a clock with the -s option. This will display the clock with the seconds hand running. Then suspend the clock with the Ctrl Z sequence. The seconds hand will stop, as the process has been suspended. Now place the process in the background with "bg" and the seconds hand will start again, and you will get your prompt back.

```
ltahoe% clock -s
         (clock will appear, seconds hand moving)
Ctrl Z
Stopped
         (clock is not running now)
ltahoe%
ltahoe% bg
ltahoe%
```

The clock is now running again.

5-5 Using the **ps** Command

The "**ps**" command (process status) will show you the current status of jobs running in the background. The **ps** command by itself will show you all of the processes you have started since you logged onto the system. This will include all processes like shelltools, commandtools, mailtool, etc.

Try the **ps** command at the command line.

```
        ltahoe% ps
118 co I    0:03 sunview
126 co I    0:01 mailtool
132 co I    0:01 textedit
135 co I    0:00 clock
120 p0 I    0:02 cmdtool
121 p0 I    0:00 -bin csh (csh)
122 p1 R    1:09 shelltool
123 p1 S    0:01 -bin csh (csh)
195 p1 R    0:00 ps
124 p2 S    3:41 shelltool
125 p2 I    0:00 -bin csh (csh)
130 p2 S    0:00 vi commands
133 p3 I    0:01 cmdtool
134 p3 I    0:00 -bin csh (csh)
ltahoe%
```

Notice that the output shows the ps command you just ran as well as the vi session.

The **ps** command can show you specific information about the status of certain processes. If you look at the first three columns, you see the following:

Process ID number   TTY port   STATUS

The process ID is the number the system assigns to the process. This is the number you will use when you wish to "kill" a process. (You will look at killing processes in a moment).

The TTY port is the system port the process is running under. In the instance of port p2, it is running a shelltool, which is running a shell, which is running vi.

The STATUS is the current state of the process. The most frequently seen process states are:

R   Process is running
S   Process is sleeping (waiting for the system to finish something else.)
I   Processes which are idle, sleeping for more than 20 seconds.

5-6 Killing Processes

You can stop a backgrounded process with the "**kill**" command. This command accepts process ID numbers as arguments. An example would be if you wanted to kill the clock listed in the ps output listed earlier. You would enter at the prompt, **kill** followed by the process ID number.

```
ltahoe% kill 135
ltahoe%
```

The clock would then disappear because its process was killed by the system.

There are several types of kill signals the system can send to terminate or alter a command. These are numbered 1 through 31 and can do many things. Most are very confusing and are never used by the average user. The one most used is -9. Since some processes ignore the standard kill signal, the -9 signal will kill even the most stubborn processes and cannot be ignored. Only use this option if the regular kill did not do the trick.

```
ltahoe% kill -9 135
```

5-7 Redirection of Standard Output

When working with most commands, the results of the command are usually displayed on the screen. This is referred to as the Standard Output. If you perform the ls command, the screen will display the contents of a directory. But what if you wish to take that output and direct it into a file? When you wish to do this you are said to "redirect" the output. The redirection character is the ">".

Try a practical example. Try doing an ls of the / file system and redirecting the output to a file called testfile.

```
ltahoe% ls -l / > testfile
ltahoe% more testfile
total 1152
lrwxrwxrwx   1 root         7 Oct 14    1988 bin ->usr/bin
-r--r--r--   1 root    126056 Oct 15    1988 boot
drwxr-sr-x   2 bin       3584 Jan 28   17:00 dev/
drwxr-sr-x   5 root      2048 Jan 28   17:00 etc/
drwxr-sr-x   4 root       512 Oct 15    1988 export/
drwxr-xr-x  11 root       512 Nov 30   15:13 home/
-rwxr-xr-x   1 root    135043 Oct 15    1988 kadb*
```

```
lrwxrwxrwx   1 root          7 Oct 14      1988 lib -> usr/lib
drwxr-xr-x   2 root       8192 Oct 14      1988 lost+found/
drwxr-sr-x   2 bin         512 Apr  9      1988 mnt/
drwxr-sr-x   2 bin         512 Oct 15      1988 sbin/
lrwxrwxrwx   1 root         15 Oct 14      1988 sys ->./usr/share
lrwxrwxrwx   1 root          9 Oct 17      1988 tmp -> /home/tmp/
drwxr-sr-x  20 root        512 Nov 30     13:46 usr/
drwxr-sr-x   9 bin         512 Apr  9      1988 var/
-rwxr-xr-x   1 root     859720 Dec  8      1988 vmunix*
```

As you can see, you did not view the results of the ls on the screen, but a new file was created called testfile which did contain the results.

Note: If you redirect the standard output to an existing file, the system will overwrite the existing file. This is because the system first creates an empty file for the output to go to. If the file is already there, the system will write over it. There is a variable called "noclobber" which prevents the system from clobbering existing files with file redirection. The noclobber variable is described in Chapter 7 on the section for your Home Directory.

5-8 Redirecting and Appending

If you want to add information to an existing file, you can append the new information by adding an additional ">" character to the string.

```
ltahoe% pwd >> testfile
ltahoe% more testfile
total 1152
lrwxrwxrwx   1 root          7 Oct 14      1988 bin -> usr/bin
-r--r--r--   1 root     126056 Oct 15      1988 boot
drwxr-sr-x   2 bin        3584 Jan 28     17:00 dev/
drwxr-sr-x   5 root       2048 Jan 28     17:00 etc/
drwxr-sr-x   4 root        512 Oct 15      1988 export/
drwxr-xr-x  11 root        512 Nov 30     15:13 home/
-rwxr-xr-x   1 root     135043 Oct 15      1988 kadb*
lrwxrwxrwx   1 root          7 Oct 14      1988 lib -> usr/lib
drwxr-xr-x   2 root       8192 Oct 14      1988 lost+found/
drwxr-sr-x   2 bin         512 Apr  9      1988 mnt/
drwxr-sr-x   2 bin         512 Oct 15      1988 sbin/
lrwxrwxrwx   1 root         15 Oct 14      1988 sys -> . /usr/share
lrwxrwxrwx   1 root          9 Oct 17      1988 tmp -> /home/tmp/
drwxr-sr-x  20 root        512 Nov 30     13:46 usr/
```

```
drwxr-sr-x  9 bin       512 Apr  9    1988 var/
-rwxr-xr-x  1 root   859720 Dec  8    1988 vmunix*
/home/ltahoe/miker
```

Notice the output of pwd was placed at the end of the file.

5-9 Redirection of Standard Input

You have seen how the > and >> can take the standard output and redirect it to a file. Now let's see how you can take the standard input and redirect it to a command.

Redirecting the standard input is accomplished with the "<" character.

Let's create a new file called datefile which will contain the current date.

ltahoe% **date > datefile**

Now you can look at the file by directing the input of the file to the more command.

ltahoe% **more < datefile**
Sun Jan 28 19:05:07 PST 1990
ltahoe%

5-10 Using the **Grep** Command

The **grep** command (Global Regular Expression Printer) is a wonderful command for finding words or patterns in a file. There are so many ways to use **grep** that you will only look at how to use it in the generic sense. By reading the man page on grep, you will find out just how powerful grep can be.

To find any match of the word *Mike* in a file called *phonelist*, you would simply enter the command:

```
ltahoe% grep Mike phonelist
Mike408-555-1212
ltahoe%
```

Note: Grep is case sensitive. If you are looking for words that start with upper case, you need to use upper case. There is an option to grep (-i) which will ignore the case of letters.

The system has now displayed any line in the file which contained the name *Mike*. If you had more than one file which you would like to search, you can specify more than one file. The system would search the named files and display the name of the file, followed by any lines which contained the pattern you are "greping" for.

```
ltahoe% grep Mike phonelist phonelist.old
phonelist:    Mike 408-555-1212
phonelist.old:Mike 415-555-1212
ltahoe%
```

If no match is found, the system will return your prompt. You can also search for a string of words by enclosing them in " ". If you wanted to search for the string *George Bush* in my *phonelist* file, you would enter the command:

```
ltahoe% grep "George Bush" phonelist
George Bush home residence 412-555-1212
George Bush work          512-555-1212
ltahoe%
```

There are some interesting options to grep. One of them is the -v option. This option to grep will display everything but the specified pattern. By redirecting the output to another file name, you can update files without ever editing them. Let's say George is no longer needed in the `phonelist` file. You can use the -v option to grep and remove him.

```
ltahoe% grep -v "George Bush" phonelist > newphonelist
```

If you grep for *George* in the new *phonelist* file called *new-phonelist*, George will not be in the file.

```
ltahoe% grep "George Bush"   newphonelist
ltahoe%
```

5-11 Connecting Commands with Pipes

Many commands produce an output which can be used by other commands to accomplish a final task. Rather than execute several command lines, you can direct the output of one command to the input of another command. This is referred to as "piping". To accomplish this you will use the "|" symbol.

A good example of piping might be to list the contents of a

large directory which contains more than one screen of output. You would like to be able to look at each screenfull of information, but the ls command just scrolls right on by you. If only you could use the **more** command on the output of the ls command you would be in good shape. This is exactly what piping can do for you. All you have to do is pipe the ouput of **ls** to the **more** command.

    ltahoe% **ls -l more**

The system would perform the **ls -l** command and pass the standard ouput to the **more** command, which in turn will only display one screenfull of information at a time.

You can also have multiple pipes on the same command line.

    ltahoe% **more phonelist | grep miker | lpr**

Here you have taken the contents of the file called phonelist and passed it on to the **grep** command, which will find the line which contains miker and then send it to the line printer.

5-12 Using the History List

The C-Shell has a capability which allows you to re-execute commands without having to enter them again. You can also specify previous command values and manipulate them on the current command line.

When you set up your *.cshrc* file, you specified a variable called "history". In the home directory example you set the history variable to 40. This means that the system will store the last 40 commands you entered into a list. Think of this list as a kind of flight recorder. You can call up this list with the history command.

```
ltahoe% history
1 ls
2 pwd
3 cd /home/miker
4 ls /home/miker
5 more testfile
```

You can now see the last five commands that were entered on the command line. The list will continue to forty commands and then start bumping off the first commands as more are entered. In this way, the "last" forty commands are stored.

Now that you have this list, what can you do with it?

5-13 Selecting Items from the History List

To call up previously entered commands, you use the "!" symbol. (Usually called "bang".) This symbol stands for: "Go to the history list." From the history list you can then re-execute commands by specifying either the number of the command, or the first letter of the command. Here are some examples using the ouput of your history listing in the previous section.

```
ltahoe% history
1 ls
2 pwd
3 cd /home/miker
4 ls /home/miker
5 more testfile
ltahoe% !4
ls /home/miker
....output of the ls command
ltahoe% !l
ls /home/miker
....output of the ls command
```

So you were able to re-run the ls command in two different ways; one with the history command number, the other with the first letter of the command.

Note: When using the first letter of the command from the history list, it will take the last command executed that started with that letter.

If you just wanted to re-execute the last command, you would enter two "!". If the last command was to ls */home/miker*, and you wanted to run this command again, you would enter:

```
ltahoe% !!
ls /home/miker
....output of the ls command
```

Using the $ with History

You now know how to access the history list and call up previous commands. Now let's try to use a part of a previous command in the current command.

You can take the last word on a command line and place it on the current command line with the "$" symbol. If you wanted to look at a file called *phonelist*, and then print it to a line printer, you can use the history list to enter the file name without having to re-enter the full file name.

```
ltahoe% more phonelist
....output from more
ltahoe% lpr !$
lpr phonelist
ltahoe%
```

Thus on the current command line, you went to the history list and took the last word from the last command, and substituted it onto the current command line. This can save a lot of typing when working with the same file or directory.

Changing a Previous Command

You can change a filename or a mistype in the previous command with the " ˆ " symbol. To subsitute a word in the previous command, place the old word in between the " ˆ " symbols and then the new word.

```
ltahoe% more phonelst
no such file or directory
ltahoe% ˆphonelistˆphonelist
more phonelist
....output from more
ltahoe%
```

5-14 Setting the Date

The **date** command, if no argument is specified, will display the current date and time. Otherwise, the date and time can be set. (ONLY THE SUPERUSER CAN CHANGE OR SET THE DATE)

To display the current date and time, enter the command:

```
ltahoe% date
```

The response would look like this:

```
ltahoe%date
Sun Oct 1 19:02:59 PDT 1989
```

If you wish to set the date and time you must become the superuser, or root.

The command line syntax for the **date** command is:

ltahoe# **date** [yymmddhhmm.ss]

Where the yy=year, mm=month, dd=day, hh=hour, mm=minutes, and .ss=seconds. The yy is optional as the year would probably already be in the system. If you need to enter the year, you only need to enter the last two digits of the year.

To set the system date to be December 25 1989 11:59 PM You would use the following command: (Be sure to be root.)

ltahoe# **date 12251159**

The response from the system would be:

```
ltahoe# date 12251159
Mon Dec 25 11:59:00 PST 1989
```

There is a "-u" option for displaying the date in GMT (universal time). The system normally uses GMT and the date command converts this to the standard time. The "-u" option can also be used to set the GMT time.

5-15 Checking Disk Space with **df**

The "**df**" command is used to report the amount of free disk space left on currently mounted file systems. The output displays the file system, the amount of space the file system has, how much has been used, how much is left available, and the percentage of the disk's total capacity that has been used. Here is a sample output of a workstation which has two disks attached, sd0 and sd1:

```
ltahoe% df
Filesystem    kbytes    used     avail    capacity   Mounted on
/dev/sd0a     7508      3189     3568     47%        /
/dev/sd0g     59147     58737    0        110%       /usr
/dev/sd1g     84130     51796    23921    68%        /home
/dev/sd1h     1162      7087     2958     71%        /var
```

You will notice several discrepancies with the addition of the numbers on each line. The amount available and the amount used do not add up to the total amount of kbytes for the disk device. This is due to the fact that the system saves 10% of the disk space for administration functions. You will also notice that the capacity can exceed 100%. This happens when the system is using the extra 10% of the "reserve" disk space.

The **df** command will also display the amount of space left on remotely mounted file systems. Please see the chapter on Networking for a description of mounting remote file systems. Here is a sample of the **df** command with file systems mounted on remote workstations:

```
ltahoe% df
```

```
Filesystem        kbytes        used        avail    capacity   Mounted on
/dev/sd0a          7508         3189         3568       47%      /
/dev/sd0g         59147        58737            0      110%      /usr
/dev/sd1g         84130        51796        23921       68%      /home
/dev/sd1h         11162         7087         2958       71%      /var
pool:/export/local/sun4-4.0
                 842171       296377       512107       37%      /usr/local
pool:/export/local/share
                 842171       296377       512107       37%      /usr/local/share
scotch:/export/ssd/sun4-4.0
                 839320       723485        31903       96%      /usr/local/ssd
forestlawn:/home/unb/doctools
                 129343        65935        50473       57%      /usr/doctools
```

The output shows the local disks and the mounted file systems at the end. The list shows the system names, followed by the file systems which are being mounted, and the directory to which they are mounted on.

5-16 Checking Disk Usage with **du**

The **du** command will enable you to check on the amount of disk space a particular directory is using. This is useful since the df command will only show you an entire file system. The output is in kbytes. To use the du command, simply enter the command "**du**", followed by the directory you wish to check.

```
ltahoe% du /tmp/junkdir
37      /tmp/junkdir
```

If you give a directory name which contains sub-directories, the output will include these as well.

You can get summaries of large directories with the -s option to **du.** The summary will not display all of the sub-directories but will add them all up for you and display a total. Here is an example of the -s option:

```
ltahoe% du -s /home/ltahoe/miker
5799    /home/ltahoe/miker
```

In this instance my home directory has close to 6 MB of data. Remember the output is in kbytes!

5-17 Looking up Words with **look**

You can check the spelling of many words with the "**look**" command. This command will take the first few letters of a word and compare them with similar words in the system dictionary located under the directory /usr/dict. To use the look command, simply enter the command **look**, followed by the first few letters of the word you wish to verify the spelling on. If you were trying to spell the word simultaneous, you would enter the command:

```
ltahoe% look simul
simulate
simulcast
simultaneity
simultaneous
ltahoe%
```

The **look** command is very useful when you are writing text and do not wish to continually look up words in a dictionary.

Editors

6

Visual Editor **VI**

This chapter will show you how to use the visual editor. It is probably the most common editor used today. It is an interactive editor which allows you not only to create files, but work with the file to perform tasks such as searching for text, reading in other files, substituting text throughout the file, and many other file editing functions.

There are as many functions to vi as there are keys on the keyboard. Virtually every key has some meaning in vi. In this chapter you will cover only the basic functions of vi because vi is so extensive in functionality that entire books are written on this subject. Refer to the guide at the end of this chapter to see some of the many options that are available in vi.

6-1 Creating a File with **vi**

To create a new file with **vi,** simple enter at the command line **vi,** followed by the new filename you wish to create.

```
ltahoe% vi junk
```

The system will now clear the window you are currently working in and bring up the vi screen. (See Figure 6.1.)

The vi screen is now up and is full of ~ characters. This tells the user the difference between the end of the file and a blank line. In this picture, the entire screen is empty with no blank lines.

If you wanted to edit an existing file, simply enter the command **vi** followed by the filename you wish to edit.

```
ltahoe% vi filename
```

You can also edit more than one file in the same vi session. To do this, enter the command **vi,** followed by the names of the files you wish to edit. Vi will edit each file, one at a time, then when you exit, vi will move to the next file that was entered on the command line.

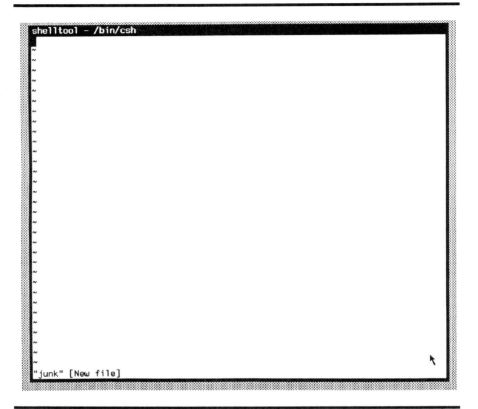

```
shelltool - /bin/csh
~
~
~
~
~
~
~
~
~
~
~
~
~
~
~
~
~
~
~
~
~
~
~
~
~
~
"junk" [New file]
```

FIGURE 6.1. *The vi screen.*

ltahoe% **vi file1 file2 file3**

If you wish to move to the next file while still in the current file, enter a :n . This will place you in the next file to be edited.

6-2 Inserting Text

Here you are ready to insert text. To insert text into a file, you must tell vi how you want to insert text. There are several ways to insert text. You will start with the (**i**) command. The i stands for insert and will insert text at the cursor. Enter the insert mode by typing an **i**. Now you are ready to enter text. Enter the following text:

This is a test file to show me how to
enter text in vi. To stop entering text,
I must hit the **esc** (escape) key.

Use these lines to practice some of the
many functions in vi.

```
shelltool - /bin/csh
This is a test file to show me how to
enter text in VI. To stop entering text,
I must hit the esc (escape) key.
Use these lines to practice some of the
many functions in VI
~
~
~
~
~
~
~
~
~
~
~
~
~
~
~
~
~
~
~
"junk" [New file]
```

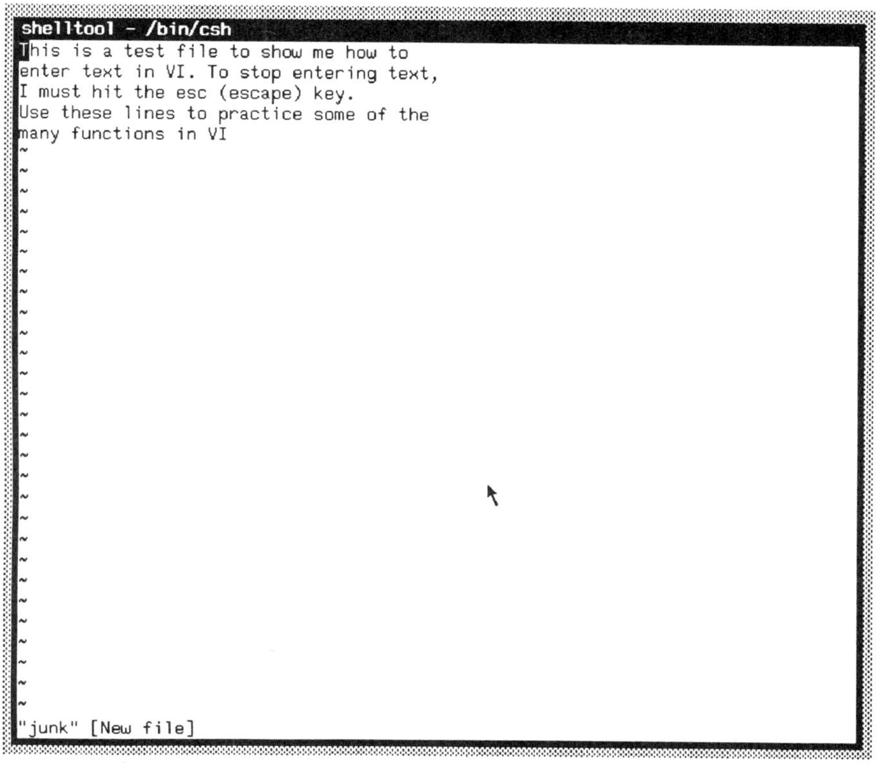

FIGURE 6.2. *vi screen with junk file text.*

Hit the escape key and you will be out of the insert mode. The escape key will remove you from the insert mode and place you back into the command mode. The command mode allows you to perform functions like moving around in the file and searching for text. There are many ways to insert text in a file. Here is a list of ways:

a	add text after the cursor
i	insert text at the cursor
I	insert text at the beginning of the line
o	open a new line under the existing line
	(this will place you in the insert mode)
O	open a new line above the current line

Remember, whenever you are finished entering text, you MUST enter the **esc** or escape key to exit the text insert mode.

6-3 Moving Around in the File

Now that you have some text in your file, you must learn how to move around in the file. This can be done in two ways. The first is the arrow keys located on the right side of the keyboard. You can use these keys to move the cursor anywhere in the file. Note that you cannot move the cursor to a position where there is neither text or a blank line. The second method to moving around in the file is to use the following four keys:

h	move the the left
j	move down
k	move up
l	move the the right

Although the arrow keys may seem easier, most users tend to use the **h, j, k,** and **l** keys so they do not have to to move their right hand off of the home position on the keyboard. Practice moving around with the two different methods and get a feel for the keys.

To move the the cursor forward one screenful, enter a **ctrl f.** If you want to move one screenful back, enter a **ctrl b.** If you want to move one half screen back, enter a **ctrl u.** If you want to move one half screen forward, enter a **ctrl d.**

6-4 Deleting Text

As with inserting text, there are many ways to delete text. While in the insert mode, you would only have to press the delete key to correct a mistake. When in the command mode, you can delete text in several ways. You can delete a single character with the (x) key, or an entire word with (dw). Here are several ways to delete text in vi:

x	delete one character
#x	delete specified number (#) of characters
X	delete previous character
#X	delete specified number (#) of previous characters
dw	delete word
#dw	delete specified number (#) of words
D	delete from cursor to end of line

dd   delete entire line
#dd   delete specified number (#) of lines

Try to use some of these commands on your junk file. Try moving the cursor onto a word and deleting a single letter, then try the entire word or line. Remember, you must be in the command mode to use these functions.

6-5 Substituting Text

Now that you can delete text, you will learn to substitute some text. Move the cursor over the word "hit" in your file and and enter the command (**cw**). This stands for change word. A **$** will appear at the end of the word. Enter the new word "press" and then hit the **esc** key. The new word press, will now replace the old word hit. When ever you enter a substitute command, vi will automatically place you in the insert mode. The substitute command will terminate when you press the **esc** key. Here is a list of substitute commands:

cw   change word
r   replace character
R   Replace characters until esc is pressed
s   Substitutes one character for what ever
            you enter.
S   Deletes entire line, then subs new text

Global substitutions can be done with the : command. If you wanted to change every instance of a word to a different word, you can use the :, followed by this method.

:**%s**/**oldpattern**/**newpattern**/**g**

If you spelled the same word wrong many places in a file, you can correct every instance of the work with this command. Try each of the substitute commands to familiarize yourself with each one.

6-6 Searching for Text

In vi you can search for a specified string of text with the / command. This command will look for the text which follows the /. In your junk file, enter a /, then type practice. Hit return and the cursor will move to the beginning of the work practice. Try it again, this time enter a /, followed by the word enter. The cursor will now move the beginning of the word enter on the second line. You can go to the next instance of the word enter by typing an **n** for next.

The cursor will move to the next instance of the word enter. Here are the commands used in searching for text.

/	search forward for a string
n	look for next instance in file
?	search backwards in a file

6-7 Joining Two Lines

You can join two lines together with the **J** command. This will take the next line and join it with the current line. Try to join two lines in your file. If the new line goes off of the current line to the next, move the cursor to where you wish the line to end, then hit **i**, followed by a return. This will end the existing line and move the rest of the text to the next line.

6-8 Undoing a Change

If you make a mistake while performing a change, you can undo the change with the **u** and **U** command. Let's say you change a word and the realize you want the old word. You can undo the last change by entering a **u.** If you enter another command after the mistake, undo will not work on the mistake since it only undo's the last command. The **U** command will undo all changes made to the current line.

6-9 Exiting a vi File

When exiting vi, you can do many things. You can write the file and continue on, you can write then exit vi, you can write then edit a new file. Here are some ways to exit vi.

ZZ	Saves and exits vi
:w	writes file without exiting
:wq	writes file and exits vi (same as ZZ)
:wq!	forces writing of file then exits
:q	exits file without writing
:q!	forces exit of file without writing

6-10 Reading in a File

If you are editing a file and wish to include another file, you can use the "r" command from the command mode. Let's say you are editing a file and you wish to include a file called data. Position the cursor where you wish the file to be added, then enter a **:r** followed by the name of the file you wish to include. (In this case, **:r** *data*). Hit the return key and the file will be read into the existing vi file. This is useful when you need to include existing text and do not wish to type it in manually.

6-11 Overview of vi Commands

Here is a list of many of the commands available in vi. Read each one and try to use it. The best way to learn vi is to practice with each command on a junk or test file. If you make a mistake in vi, the screen will flash and beep.

TABLE OF vi COMMANDS

COMMAND		FUNCTION
A		add text at end of line
a		Append text from cursor point.
b		Move to beginning of word where cursor is positioned or move cursor back one word.
#b		Move cursor back # words. **
C		Change from cursor point to end of the line.
cw		Change word.
<control> b		Move window backward through the file.
<control> d		Scroll down half window.
<control> f		Move window forward through the file.
<control> u		Scroll up half window.
<control> h		Move cursor one character to the left (backspace).
<control> n		Move cursor to the next line.
<control> p		Move cursor to the previous line.
<control> z		Puts vi file in the background and returns to shell, return to file by using fg shell command.
<space>		Move cursor one character to right.
df		Delete up to and including character (syntax dfx)*
dw		Delete word (5dw would delete 5 words).
D		Delete from cursor point to end of line. ***
dd		Delete complete line (5dd would delete 5 lines). ***
e		Move to end of word cursor is positioned on.
F		Search back on line for character (syntax Fx)*
f		Search forward on line for character (syntax fx)*
G		Go to the bottom of the file.
G	also	Go to specified number (syntax # G)**
H		Home (Top of window)
h		Move cursor left.
I		Insert text at the beginning of the line.
i		Insert text from the cursor point.
J		Join the preceding line with the current line.
#J		Join the preceding # of lines with the current line.

j	Move cursor down.
k	Move cursor up.
L	Go to the last line of the file.
#L	Go to #'th line from the bottom of the file.
l	Move cursor right.
m	Marks a position, 'm returns to that position.
M	Moves cursor to middle line of the screen.
N	Find next string in reverse direction (See /)
n	Find next string in same direction (See /)
O	Open a line above the current line.
o	Open a line below the current line.
P	Put text above the current line.
p	Put text below the current line.
R	Replace characters until escape is received.
r	Replace character at cursor point.
s	Substitute text until escape is received
T	Same as F except cursor placed to left of specified character
t	Same as f except cursor placed to left of specified character
U	Undo all changes made on current line
u	Undo last change
W	Move forward to beginning of next character string
w	Move forward to beginning of next word.
X	Delete previous character.
#X	Delete previous # of characters.
x	Delete character at cursor position.
#x	Delete # of characters beginning with cursor position
y	Yank—can be used in conjunction with numbers and other commands (For example, y2f yanks everything from the cursor position to the second following semicolon.)
Y	Yank the line (See also, P-put)
z<CR>	Makes current line the top of the screen.
z-	Makes current line the bottom of the screen.
'	Deletes whole lines from the current line up to and including the marked position.
.	Repeat last command.
/	Search forwards in the file. (Note: when searching for a string beginning with /, you must escape the string's / with a /).
`	Deletes from the current cursor position up to, but not including the marked position.
?	Search backwards in the file.
!	Escape (Example, !csh escapes to shell, then exit returns to file.

ˆ	Move cursor to beginning of line
$	Move cursor to end of current line.
\<Esc\>	Escape the vi command.
:s	Substitute.
:n	Move to the next file.
:r FILENAME	Recall FILENAME and insert at cursor position in current file. (:r without FILENAME inserts a copy of the current file).
:#	Go to specified line number.
ZZ	Save and exit file
:wq	Save and exit file
:wq!	Force save and exit file (Example, use when the file is owned by you but is read only)
:w	Write file but do not exit.
:w!	Force write of file but do not exit.
:q	Quit file without saving.
:q!	Force Quit file without saving (Example, use when the file has been edited since opened, but you still want to quit without saving the changes)
~	Change case on character at cursor position.

* x being the named character
** # being the specified number
*** Note that deleted lines can be "put" somewhere else (see P,p)

Defaults Editor
What Is the Defaults Editor?

The defaults editor is a SunView application that provides a simple and convenient method of viewing and changing default parameters of your working environment. The UNIX operating system is infinitely configurable. It is literally possible to customize your environment to the point that others might not recognize that you are running UNIX. The standard way of "personalizing" your environment was by modifying parameters in a number of different 'dot' files (*.cshrc*, *.login*, *.mailrc* etc). Like so much of earlier versions UNIX, it was very easy to shoot yourself in the foot. The defaults editor provides a tool to make the job considerably easier, with most of the hazard removed.

6-12 Running the Defaults Editor

The defaults editor is most often invoked from the root menu.

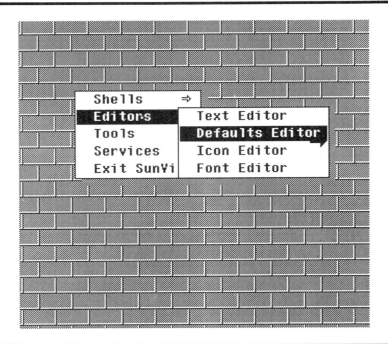

FIGURE 6.3. *Rootmenu selection of the defaults editor.*

Alternatively, the defaults editor can be run from the command line as a background process. Backgrounding a job tells the system to take control of the process rather than the current window you are working in. Background processes were discussed in Section 5-4.

    ltahoe% **defaultsedit &**

Using the "&" makes the shelltool available for other uses by placing the job in the background. When invoked, the defaults editor looks like Figure 6.4.

6-13 General Description

The defaults editor consists of four subwindows. From top to bottom they are:

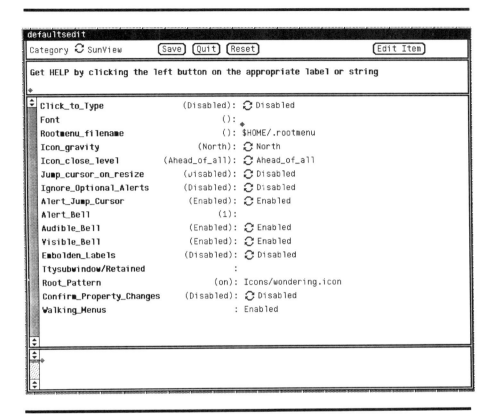

```
defaultsedit
Category ↻ SunView          (Save) (Quit) (Reset)                    (Edit Item)

Get HELP by clicking the left button on the appropriate label or string
◆
  Click_to_Type              (Disabled): ↻ Disabled
  Font                              (): ◆
  Rootmenu_filename                 (): $HOME/.rootmenu
  Icon_gravity                 (North): ↻ North
  Icon_close_level       (Ahead_of_all): ↻ Ahead_of_all
  Jump_cursor_on_resize     (Disabled): ↻ Disabled
  Ignore_Optional_Alerts    (Disabled): ↻ Disabled
  Alert_Jump_Cursor          (Enabled): ↻ Enabled
  Alert_Bell                       (1):
  Audible_Bell               (Enabled): ↻ Enabled
  Visible_Bell               (Enabled): ↻ Enabled
  Embolden_Labels           (Disabled): ↻ Disabled
  Ttysubwindow/Retained              :
  Root_Pattern                    (on): Icons/wondering.icon
  Confirm_Property_Changes  (Disabled): ↻ Disabled
  Walking_Menus                      : Enabled
```

FIGURE 6.4. *The defaults editor screen with sunview menu selected.*

Control	This window contains the name of the category currently displayed in Parameters window, and the buttons Save, Quit, Reset, and Edit Item.
Message	This is a small text subwindow used by the defaults editor to display messages of interest about the category and item chosen in the parameters window.
Parameters	This window shows the current parameters for the category selected in the control window. Clicking the left mouse button over a parameter will display a help message in the message window. Note, not all parameters will have help messages associated with them. this is especially true of parameters that you have added.
Edit	This is a small text subwindow, a scratchpad in essence, which enables text editing of parameter values. This is extremely useful when dealing with long or complicated values, such as mailing lists or printer filters.

6-14 Control Subwindow

Category   There are two ways of changing the displayed category. You can cycle through the available categories by clicking on the left button anywhere near the arrows. Alternatively, you can bring up a submenu by pressing the right button, and selecting the desired category.

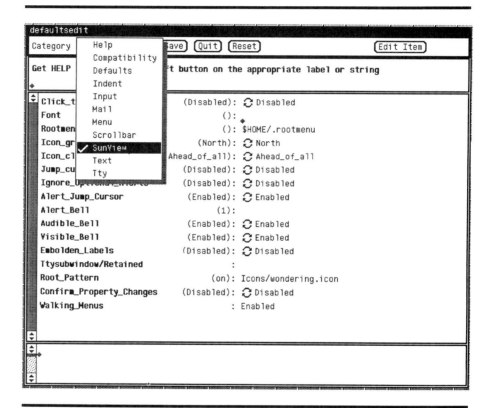

FIGURE 6.5. *Selecting alternate menus with the catagory submenu.*

Save   Click left on the save button to save the changes made in this editing session. The values that you have changed will be saved in your .defaults file in your home directory.

Quit   Exit without saving changes. Select with the left mouse button.

Reset   Clicking left on the reset button will reset the values in the displayed category to that of your private defaults database. This is a limited use "undo" function. Once you have "saved" the values, a reset will no longer work.

Edit Item The Edit Item is used to modify lines in the parameter window. It is rarely used by most users, and only one example will be provided in this chapter.

6-15 Cycling Through the Categories

Mail The mail category is one of the most extensive, and probably one of the categories that you will use the most. As its name implies, the mail category allows you to change the way you do certain things within mail and mailtool.

Menu The Menu category affects the appearance of menus, what happens to the pointer after you choose an item, and even how you select an item. Again, this is a category that you will use a lot until you have decided what works best for you.

Scrollbar The scrollbar category is by far one of the most fun to use. It even comes with a popup program so you can see the affect of changes as they occur.

SunView This is where you make changes global to the SunView environment such as the default font.

Text The Text category lets you modify the behavior of text windows. This is especially important for modifying the behavior of Textedit.

Indent The Indent category sets the defaults for the indent command. The 'Pretty Print C' command from the root menu is affected by the Indent defaults.

Input You use the Input category to change the defaults associated with mouse and keyboard interaction.

Defaults The defaults category is used to change the defaults of the defaults editor itself, and is rarely used by anyone but programmers.

Tty The Tty category lets you change a few of the characteristics of your terminal and command windows, but is rarely used by the new user.

Compatibility This category lets you change the SunView defaults to those of the previous release. This is mainly to provide backwards compatibility.

Help Modify the location of the *.info files used by the help-viewer (rarely used).

6-16 Defaults Explanation

First, it would take far too long to list all of the defaults and what they do. Plus, that would take the fun out of experimenting with your environment, and making it just the way you want it. Still, to help you get started, you will go over some of the more common categories, and the defaults therein.

Note: This will not be an exhaustive listing, but rather more of push in the direction of experimentation. Don't be afraid to try your changes out. The worst that will happen is you don't like the way things work after you change them, and you'll just have to put things back the way they were. Just remember to jot down what defaults you have changed and put them back the way they were if you don't like them. In the meantime, by experimenting, you'll get a much clearer idea of how Sun's systems in general work.

When the defaults editor is first invoked, it displays the SunView category, lets start there.

SunView

Click-to-Type Catagory Click to type is an interesting variation on how the keyboard and mouse focus interact. When you have click to type disabled (the default), any typing you do will show up in the window that the mouse is pointing at. With click to type enabled, you can move the mouse cursor around to other windows, while any typing you do is displayed in the last window you selected. This is useful if you are mousing (moving) lots of data between windows, but it can also be a bit distracting because you have to click the left mouse button to type in another window.

Font Select a default font. Fonts are located in /usr/lib/fonts/ fixedwidthfonts. There are several sizes and styles, or by using the font editor you can create your own.

Alert-Bell How many times do you want your computer to beep/ flash at you when you make a mistake.

Visible-Bell, Audible-Bell Enabling the Visible Bell causes your screen to flash when you do something the computer doesn't understand, the Audible Bell turns on or off the beep.

Mail

There are so many different parameters to change in mail that a book could be written just on them (well, not really, but you get the idea). A great many of them will be of little or no interest to you, but there are a few that need to be mentioned.

Set/Printmail Set up how to print mail from your mailtool. This needs to be configured for the specific environment you work in. You will need to see your systems administrator to get the exact syntax, but it is important to have it correct. Otherwise, you have to jump through hoops to get your mail printed.

Set/askcc Set/asksub These two categories tell the mail program if it should ask for a subject for your mail, or a Cc: line. It is a good idea to leave the asksub at the default yes, since all the mail you send should have a subject line. The askcc is more of a personal choice. What do you prefer? Personally, I prefer that the computer always ask if I want to send carbon copies of my message to others.

Set/Folder This is the name of your folder directory (usually Mail or folders). Folders are just like folders in a file cabinet. They are convenient to use, especially from Mailtool, and you will definitely want to set them up. Be sure and make a subdirectory of the same name as you use for Set/folder.

Set/record The Set/record is the name of a file that mail will use to keep a copy of all the mail you send out. It defaults to $HOME/ mail.record ($HOME is a shortcut for your home directory). This file can become quite large, so clean it out now and then.

Menu

There is only one item of interest to the new user in this category. That is the "Stay-up". To bring up the root menu, you normally click and hold the right mouse button. If you enable

Stay-up, the first click on the right button brings up the root menu, and the second click selects the chosen item. Now of course, Stay-up is very annoying to those who don't use it, and conversely not using it is very annoying to those who do. Try both ways, and pick the one that is best for you.

Scrollbar

The scrollbar category is by far the most interesting to experiment with. This category changes the way any program that uses scrollbars will look. Even better, it comes with a pop-up program so you can try out the changes immediately. Then when you have chosen the settings that are best for you, it writes those changes back to the defaults editor. You start the scrolldefaults demo by clicking left on the button at the bottom of the parameter window.

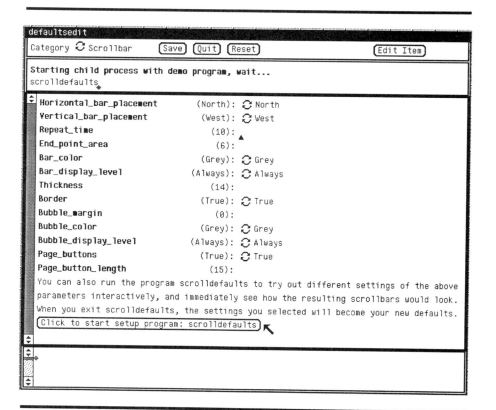

FIGURE 6.6. *The scrollbar menu.*

The scrolldefaults program looks like this.

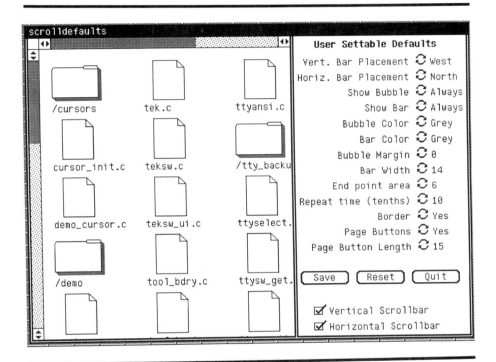

FIGURE 6.7. *The scrolldefaults menu.*

The other categories are really at this point not very interesting. If you are going to be doing a lot of C code, then you will want to look at the indent category. Other potentially interesting categories are Input and Text. You will want to refer to the appropriate manual sections for clarification of these parameters, as they are beyond the scope of this book.

Textedit

Introduction

This chapter describes how to use the textedit tool to do basic edit operations on text files.

6-17 What Is Textedit

Textedit is the window based text editor for the Sun workstation running suntools or openlook. The underlying textedit subwindow used in textedit is also used in many other window based tools, such as "cmdtool" and "mailtool". The techniques described in this chapter, such as scrolling and find, will be of use in running other window based tools.

6-18 Keyboard or Mouse

Within textedit the basic edit commands can be issued either by using the mouse, walking down menus and selecting an operation, or by the use of the specially configured keyboard keys. The keys configured for textedit are those groups of keys located on the far right and far left on the keyboard. Figure 6-8 and Figure 6-9 show the layout of keys and the edit/scrolling action associated with each individual key. On later Sun keyboards these keys are labeled, however early models of the keyboard have markings such as "L6". If these keys are not marked with their edit function labels please take the time to do so. The key labels should have come with your system in the white beginners guides. This time will be well spent and ease the use of the textedit operations.

6-19 Invoking Textedit

The texteditor can be invoked either by using the suntools/ openlook root menu and selecting the textedit item or by running the tool from the command line as follows :-

textedit &

or

textedit <filename> &

The latter method invokes textedit and automatically loads the file <filename> into the tool. The "&" causes the textedit to be run as a background process and as a result it will not lock up the window in which it was invoked. Figure 6-10 shows the menu method for invoking textedit.

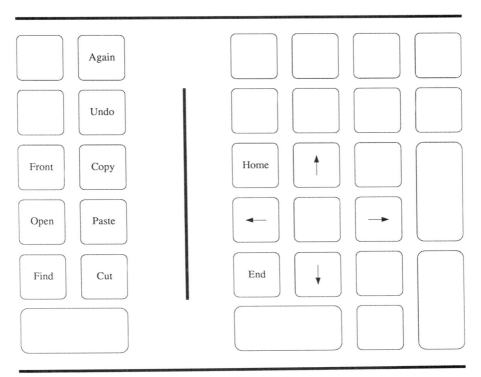

FIGURE 6.8.
Left side keyboard function keys.

FIGURE 6.9.
Right side keyboard function keys.

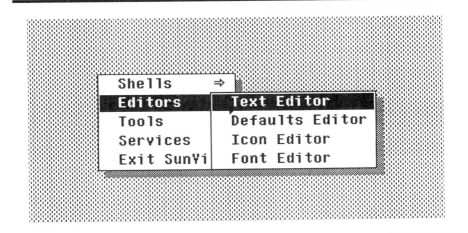

FIGURE 6.10. *Invoking the texteditor from the main sunview root menu.*

6-20 Window Layout

When textedit is invoked the textedit window will appear. Figure 6-11 illustrates a typical textedit window.

Namestripe

Scratch sub-window

Main text sub-window

Scroll bar

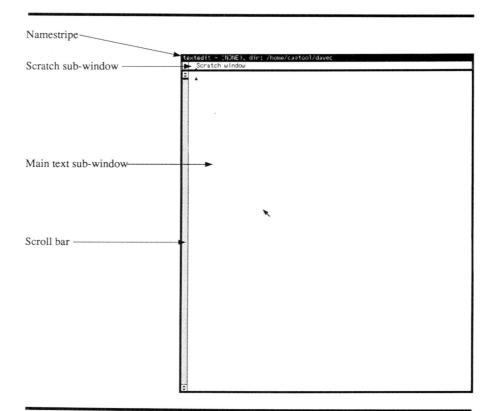

FIGURE 6.11. *Typical textedit window.*

If the textedit window is closed (by placing the mouse over the textedit window and pressing the function key "open/close") an icon is created. The name of the file currently loaded will be displayed in an icon. Similarly the icon can be re-opened by placing the mouse over the icon and pressing the function key "open/close".

The textedit window consists of:-

• A namestripe that indicates the file and directory in which the file being edited exists. The message "(edited)" is displayed after the filename if the file has been modified since it was loaded.

• A scratch sub-window. This sub-window is a window where the user can type text, without affecting the text loaded into the edit sub-window. This sub-window is useful as a temporary typing space for such operations as "find".

• The main text sub-window. This sub-window contains the file to be edited.

6-21 Loading a File

There are several ways to load a file into textedit. The simplest is to invoke textedit with a specific filename. The file is then loaded automatically into the invoked textedit window. An alternative method is to type the name of the file to be loaded into the main text sub-window and press the escape button, marked "Esc" on the keyboard. If the requested file does not exist you will hear a "beep" and an error window will appear. Files from other directories can be loaded by the same method except the full or relative pathname to the file must be specified.

6-22 Editing a New File

To start editing a new file no special action is required and the texteditor is ready for use.

6-23 Moving Around the File
Using the Mouse to Scroll

On the side of the main text sub-window is the scrollbar. The scrollbar is an important part of textedit. Figure 6-12 shows a textedit of a large file. The whole scroll bar represents the length of the file being edited. The scroll bubble indicates the part of the file that is presently visible in the text sub-window. Placing the mouse over the scrollbar and clicking the middle button will display that part of the loaded text file in the window. The scroll bubble will adjust to represent the position of the viewed text within the file.

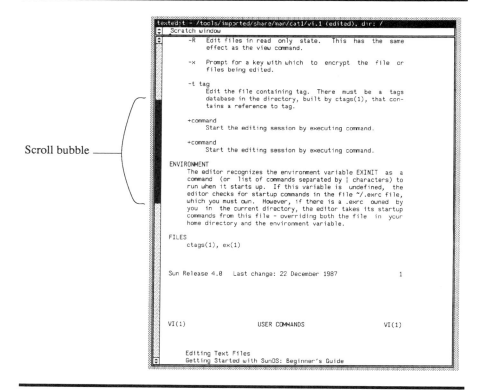

Scroll bubble

FIGURE 6.12. *Texteditor with a large file loaded.*

The displayed text can be scrolled more selectively by placing the mouse over the scroll bar and clicking on the left button to scroll up and the right button to scroll down. The actual amount of scrolling depends on the position of the mouse arrow within the scroll bar. The nearer mouse arrow is to the top of the scroll bar the lower the amount of scroll per key click.

Using the Keyboard to Scroll

The group of keys on the far right of the keyboard can also be used to move around the file. Figure 6-13 describes these keys and their functionality.

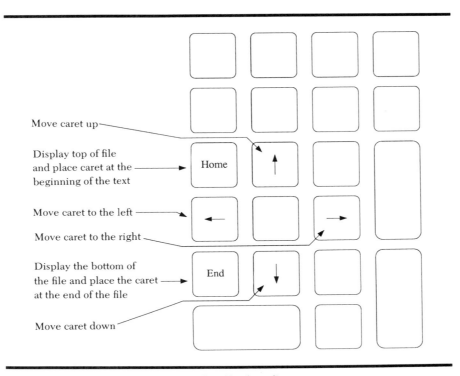

FIGURE 6.13. *Edit function keys (on right of keyboard).*

6-24 Edit Operations
Selecting Text

The majority of the textedit edit operations involve the selection of text. It is important to understand how to select text.

To select a single character place the mouse arrow over the desired character and click the left button on the mouse. Clicking the mouse twice, quickly, will select a single text word. Clicking three times will select the whole line.

A contiguous span of characters can be selected by positioning the mouse arrow over the first character and clicking the left button on the mouse. Then move the mouse arrow to the last character and click the middle button on the mouse.

In all the above instances the selected text will be highlighted in reverse video.

Figure 6-14 shows several examples of selected text.

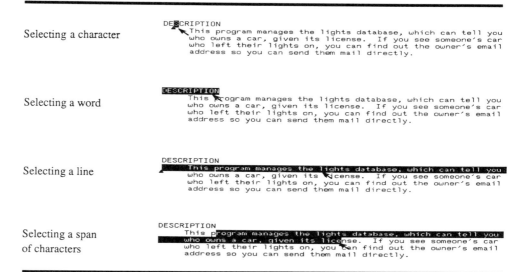

Selecting a character

Selecting a word

Selecting a line

Selecting a span
of characters

FIGURE 6.14. *Selecting text.*

Inserting Text

To insert text, position the mouse arrow at the point in the file where text is to be inserted and click the left mouse button once to select a character. Whenever text is selected a small triangle will appear at the one end of the selected text. This blinking triangle is called the caret. The caret will appear at the end of the selected text nearest to the position of the mouse arrow when the text was selected. The caret indicates the place in the text where text will be inserted. Any text typed at the keyboard will be inserted to the left of the caret.

Deleting Text

Deleting text is similar to inserting text except the delete key will delete text to the left of the caret. A more efficient method of deleting a span of characters is to select the characters to be deleted and then press the function key "Cut". The selected characters will then be deleted.

Moving Text

To move text from one position in the text file to another first select the text to be moved then press the function key "Cut". This deletes the selected text from the file. Select the required insertion point using the mouse. Then press the function key "Paste"; this will insert the deleted text to the left of the caret.

Copying Text

Similarly text can be copied, the difference being that the function key "Copy" should be used instead of the function key "Cut".

Substituting Text

To substitute text select the text to be substituted, delete this text using the function key "Cut", and then type in the new text at the keyboard.

Undo

The function key "Undo" is provided to allow the edit operations to be rolled back. For instance, if a series of edit operations have been done, but the results were unsatisfactory, the user may roll back the edit operations by repeatedly pressing the function key "Undo". Each press of the "Undo" will roll back the text file one edit operation.

Finding Text

To find specific character strings in the text file, place the mouse arrow over the scratch sub-window and type the character string. Select the typed character string, then move the mouse over the main editor sub-window and press the function key "find". The first occurrence of the selected text in the edited file will be highlighted. Repeated pressing of the function key "find" will find the second, third etc. occurrence of the selected string of characters. If no such character string can be found the whole window will blink reverse video and a "beep" will be heard.

By default the find operation will search from the beginning of the file to the end. The direction of the search can be reversed by pressing the "shift" key at the same time as the function key "find".

A find and replace dialog box can be initiated from the textedit find menu. Figure 6-16 shows the find menu and the associated dialog box.

Combinations of Edit Operations

The basic edit operations can be combined to make more complex edit operations. For instance a global substitute of a text string consists of a find command followed by typing in the substitute text. This operation can be repeated by pressing the function key "again" until all instances of the character string have been replaced.

6-25 Saving Edited Work

When the edit of the text file has been completed the file can be saved by using the "Save Current File" option of the file menu in the editor menu as shown in Figure 6-15. To store a new file, type the new file name into the scratch sub-window, select the file name, place the mouse arrow over the main edit sub-window and select the "Store as New File" option of the file menu in the editor menu as shown in Figure 6-16.

6-26 Quitting the Editor

To quit the editor position the mouse arrow over the window name stripe and select the "quit" option from the menu.

6-27 Backup Files

When a file is saved in textedit a copy of the previous contents of the file are stored in the file <filename.ext>%.

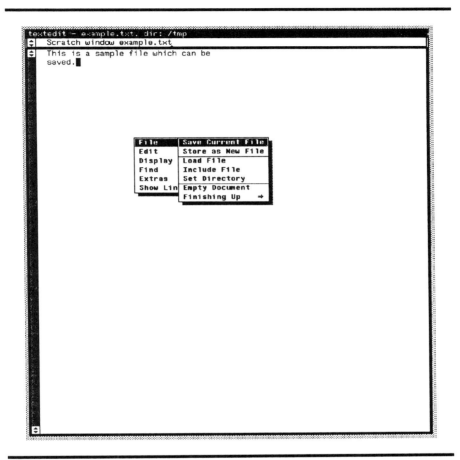

FIGURE 6.15. *Example of saving the current file with the menu.*

6-28 Other Textedit Features

Textedit has many other features. The "SunView Beginner's Guide" from Sun Microsystems is a comprehensive guide to these features. Figure 6-17 shows the main textedit menus and briefly describes their functionality.

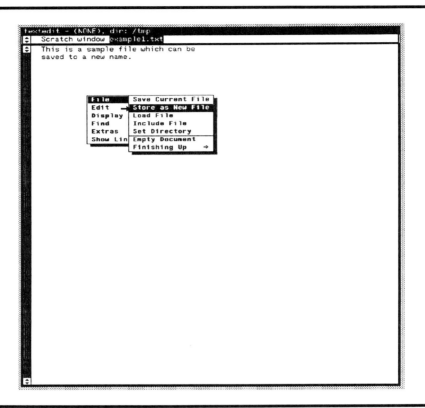

FIGURE 6.16. *Example of saving a file as a new file with the menu.*

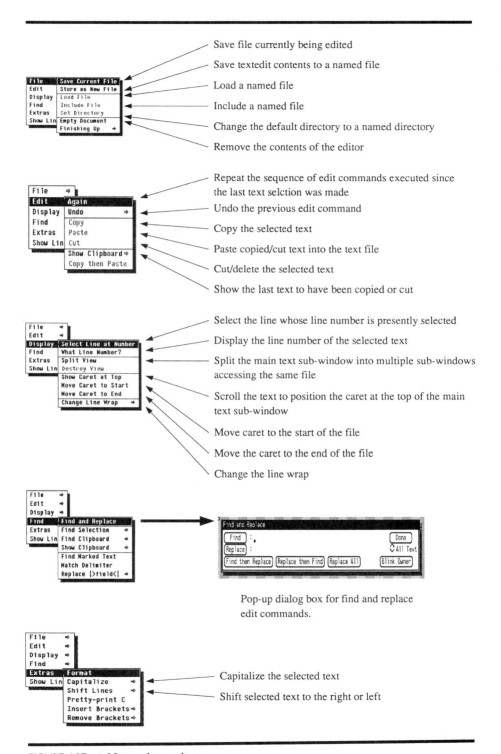

Save file currently being edited

Save textedit contents to a named file

Load a named file

Include a named file

Change the default directory to a named directory

Remove the contents of the editor

Repeat the sequence of edit commands executed since the last text selction was made

Undo the previous edit command

Copy the selected text

Paste copied/cut text into the text file

Cut/delete the selected text

Show the last text to have been copied or cut

Select the line whose line number is presently selected

Display the line number of the selected text

Split the main text sub-window into multiple sub-windows accessing the same file

Scroll the text to position the caret at the top of the main text sub-window

Move caret to the start of the file

Move the caret to the end of the file

Change the line wrap

Pop-up dialog box for find and replace edit commands.

Capitalize the selected text

Shift selected text to the right or left

FIGURE 6.17. *Additional textedit menus.*

Your Home Directory

7

7-1 General Info

For each user on a system, there will be a directory that is your home base of operations. This is the directory where you, as a user, will keep your files. Your password entry in the */etc/passwd* file points to this directory, so when you log into your system, you will be automatically placed into this directory.

Under SunOS Release 4.x, the location of your home directory should be under the directory /home. In most cases it will be located under */home/systemname/username.*

You should keep your home directory as neat as possible. This means you should store files in directories which reference the files held within. If you save files to your home directory without placing them in appropriate directories, it becomes very difficult to locate the specific file you may be looking for. For instance, do not save 12 files which represent a project directly to your home directory. Create a directory called project-x and store the files there. This way you can locate the files easily and your home directory will not display two pages of files, everytime you perform the ls command.

7-2 Dot Files

Under your home directory will be several files that control your working environments. These files are referred to as "." files or "dot files". They are called .files because they have a dot preceding them and do not show up when you use the standard ls command. They can be listed by using the -a option to ls.

The .files are system environment files that control certain aspects of the system's functionality.

The basic .files which you will look at in this section are the primary .files which all users should have.

The basic set of .files are:

.cshrc	shell environments
.login	global environments
.mailrc	mail environments
.sunview	sunview environments
.defaults	general system defaults
.rootmenu	menu attributes in sunview

You will need to edit each one of these files to customize your working environment. First let's examine the basic descriptions of each file and then you will edit them one by one. Edit the files with vi unless you know how to use another editor already. You will be referencing vi when being asked to edit a file. (See the section on vi in the Editors chapter, if you do not know how to use this editor.)

.cshrc The *.cshrc* file is the setup file for your C-Shell variables. Cshrc stands for "C-Shell-Run-Command". In this file you will "set" options and variables that you will want all shells and windows to have. There is a default .cshrc file located under /usr/lib, which you can copy into your home directory, or you could use the custom one located in this chapter.

.login This file is used for setting up global information on your system. The *.login* file is read only once at the time of login and is never looked at by the system again until the next login session. It is read after the *.cshrc* file. Here is where you will set up your terminal characteristics, default printer, and other system variables. There is a default *.login* file located under */usr/lib,* which you can copy into your home directory, or you could use the custom one located in this chapter.

.mailrc Here you will keep the information that controls the appearance of mail and the mailtool program.

.defaults From SunView you can set up many of the system attributes using the defaults editor. This file contains information relating to mail, SunView, and many other SunView applications.

.rootmenu The .rootmenu file defines what appears in the SunView menu. Here you may set up custom menus that allow you to call up applications and tools using the mouse.

.sunview This file contains all of the window attributes that appear when you enter SunView. You can use the default *.sunview* file in

/usr/lib, or you can customize your own. You will generate a custom *.sunview* file in the section on SunView.

You now know that you have a few files that you need to make. Although these files are not necessary for your system to funtion, they will make the operation of your personal environment much easier to use.

So let's start by building these .files one by one. You will begin with the *.cshrc* file.

7-3 The *.cshrc* File

As you saw earlier, the *.cshrc* file is read when you first log into the system. In the */etc/passwd* file there is a field which describes the type of shell you use. In this example you will assume that the c-shell is specified. When you log in, the */etc/passwd* file passes on what shell to use and where to find your home directory. In your home directory the system looks for the .cshrc file and "runs" the file. "Run" means that the shell reads this file and stores the information contained within. The information in the .cshrc file can range from setting the search path for commands, to renaming basic commands to include options without having to type them in.

Aliases in the *.cshrc* File

The re-naming of commands, (referred to as aliases) is a method to abbreviate long winded and commonly used commands to shorter and easier to enter command name. An example of an aliased command would be:

alias cdngm cd /home/miker/games/newgames

This alias would place me into the newgames directory by only entering the command **cdngm.**

Aliases are kept in the *.cshrc* file. You may enter any number of aliases you wish. Be careful not to create aliases using existing UNIX command names. Like aliasing the ls command: alias ls ls -als. This may cause a problem when you want to use a different option to the ls command and you have aliased it to run with these options already. As in the example, you should choose something easy to remember and not be the exact UNIX command name. You will see some other example aliases in the custom .cshrc file in this chapter.

Here is a simple .cshrc file that anyone can enter into their system. It contains many options that most users find useful. Once you get familiar with the system, you will surely be adding your own options later. After the file, you will look at each entry to see what function it performs.

You may retype this file exactly as it is here. Be careful not to make any typing mistakes or the file may not work. You can also copy the generic .cshrc file located under /usr/lib called Cshrc into your home directory.

    ltahoe% cp /usr/lib/Cshrc̄ /.cshrc

Note: The ~ symbol represents the location of your home directory. It is a default for the system. When encountered, the system substitutes the ~ symbol with the path to your home directory. (Any line that begins with a # sign, is considered a comment line, and the system does not look at that line of the file.)

A "\" (backslash) at the end of a line, tells the system that the current line continues to the next line. It is only used to make the file easier to read. A carriage return must immediately follow a backslash or the file will not work.

```
##############################################
#                    Sample .cshrc file for your home directory
#                    For interactive and noninteractive C-shells.


#
#SET UP SEARCH PATHS
#

set lpath=(\
                    /specialdir                        \
                    )

set lpath=(\
                    /usr/bin                           \
                    /usr/etc                           \
                    /usr/local                         \
                    /usr/local/bin                     \
                    /usr/doctools/bin                  \
                    /usr/doctools/lib                  \
                    -/bin                              \
                                                       \
                                                       \
                    .                                  \
                    $lpath                             \
                    $mypath                            \
                    )
```

```
set mycd=(\
                    -/bin                                    \
                    -/src                                    \
                    )

    set cdpath=(\

                    -                                        \
                    /usr/local                               \
                    $mycd                                    \
                    )

#
#                                   Set for protection of overwrites
#

set noclobber

#
#                                   Create aliases for system shells
#

alias rm            'rm -i'
alias mv            'mv -i'
alias cp            'cp -i'
umask 022

#
#                                   System will not read the rest of this file
#                                              if shell in noninteractive
#
#

if ($user == 0 || $?prompt == 0) exit

#
#                                   General settings for interactive shells
#

set history=40
set ignoreeof
set filec
set prompt=ltahoe%
#
#                                   Create aliases for your own use
#

alias ll            'ls -la'
```

```
alias st              sunview
alias mroe           more
alias page           less
alias c              clear
alias h              history \!* |head -39 |more

a sd 'echo -n "^[]l$cwd^[\"'
a cd 'cd \!* ; sd'

alias psfind         'ps -aux grep \!*|grep -v grep'
alias slay           'set j=`ps -ax|grep \!*|head -1`; kill -9 `echo $j[1]`'
alias so             source

alias lpr            'lpr -Pprintername'
alias lpq            'lpq -Pprintername'
alias lprm           'lprm -Pprintername'

alias lock           lockscreen
####################################################
                 End of .cshrc file
```

Now let's break down each item in the sample .cshrc file to find out what they really do.

```
set mypath=(\
                    -/mybin                              \
                    /specialdir                          \
                    )
```

This sets a list of search paths to special directories you may have commands in. These would be directories other than the normal UNIX command directories. You will notice the "\" at the end of some lines. This escapes or "hides" the return character. The path string must be one continuous line. Therefore you must "cover up" the carriage return so it appears to the shell that the line does not end until it observes a return character. All paths must be placed within the "( )".

```
set path=(\
                        /usr/bin                         \
                        /usr/etc                         \
                        /usr/local                       \
                        /usr/local/bin                   \
                        /usr/doctools/bin                \
                        /usr/doctools/lib                \
```

```
$lpath                                    \
$mypath                                   \
)
```

This sets the search paths to the normal UNIX commands directories. As in the previous path string there is only one search path per line, this makes it much easier to see which paths you already have when adding new additions to the search string. The last path in this string is the "$mypath" variable. You already set this variable in the previous set command. This path adds to the existing list of paths, the ones contained in "mypath".

```
set mycd=(\
        -/bin                             \
        -/src                             \
        )
```

This creates a variable that defines path names to directories that you frequently cd to. These should be the parent directories of the ones you go to. The search path is the route to local directories which you cd to frequently. It helps to eliminate typing in long paths when cd'ing to another directory.

```
set cdpath=(\
        ~                                 \
        /usr/local                        \
        $mycd                             \
        )
```

This has the same result as the previous search path except that these paths are for the standard directories you would normally cd to.

```
#
#                       Set for protection of overwrites
#

set noclobber
```

This variable protects you from accidentally overwriting a file when you use the ">" symbol. This is the redirect symbol and is used when directing output information to a filename.

```
#
#                       Create aliases for system shells
#

alias       rm      'rm -i'
```

This alias sets the interactive mode on the rm (remove) command. The system will ask you if you are sure you want to delete a file before it actually removes it. (This is recommended for new users.)

    alias   mv   'mv -i'

This alias sets the interactive mode on the mv (move) command. The system will ask you if you wish to overwrite an existing file when you use mv.

    alias   cp   'cp -i'

This alias sets up the interactive mode on the cp (copy) command. The system will ask you if you wish to overwrite existing files when you use cp.

    umask   022

This variable sets the permissions on newly created files. The permissions that would be set with the umask 022 are 644. Please refer to the section on permissions for more detailed information on "umask".

    #
    #   The system will not read the rest of this file
    #   if shell is non-interactive.
    #

    if ($user == 0 || $?prompt == 0) exit

This command finds out if the user reading this file is a real person or the system itself. The C-Shell can spawn off other shells that perform tasks. When reading this file you do not want the system to waste time reading aliases and other items that only the user needs. So if the system is reading this file for itself, then it will stop at this point. This speeds up the system when it is spawning new shells.

    #
    #   General settings for interactive shells
    #

    set history=40

Here you record the last 40 commands that were entered. You can recall these commands with the history command. (See the section on the history command) set ignoreeof

This prevents you from accidentally logging out when you type a "Ctrl-D"

set filec

This sets the file continuation variable. When entering long path names or file names, just type in the first few characters of a path or filename, and then the "esc" key. The system will enter the rest of the name for you. If there is more than one file with the same first few characters, the system will want the next character that is different in the name and will then complete the name.

set prompt=ltahoe%

Here you can set the prompt to whatever you like. In this instance, the prompt will be ltahoe%. You can set it to be the system name, which is the default, or virtually anything you can think of.

```
#
#                          Create aliases for your own use
#
```

alias   ll   'ls -la'

This aliases the ls -la command to now be "ll"

alias   sv   sunview

This is an abbreviation for the executable sunview

alias   mroe   more

This will help you from having to backspace and re-type the word more each time you type ahead of yourself and misspell it.

alias   page   less

This alias works like the more command except that it allows you to scroll backwards when you view a file.

alias   c   clear

An abbreviation for the clear screen command.

alias   h   history !* |head -39 |more

This dispays the history table but does not display the command you used to list the history table.

a sd 'echo -n "^[]l$cwd^[\"'
a cd 'cd \!* ; sd'

This set of aliases will take the output of the cd command and display it in the upper border of a SunView window. The ^[sequence is an escape funtion and is not typed as a ^[, but is entered with the control-v (esc) sequence in vi. See the section on vi for entering escape characters.

alias   psfind   'ps -aux |grep \!*|grep -v grep'

This alias finds the process id number of the name of a process you ask for.

alias   slay   'set j=`ps -ax|grep \!*|head -1`; kill -9 `echo $j[1]`'

This alias will kill a named process that is currently running.

alias   so   source

This is an abbreviation for source. You use this command after you make changes to your . (dot) files. The system only reads .files when you log in or create a new shell. If you want new changes to take effect in your current shell, you need to source the .file after you have made the edit. Only the shell you source the file in will have the changes. If you want all other shells to have the change, you will need to either log out and back in, or source each window you have running.

alias   lpr1

This aliases the lpr command so you do not have to enter the printer name of an alternate printer that is not the same as the one specified in your PRINTER variable in your .login file.

alias   lpq1   'lpq -Pprintername'

This aliases the lpq command in the same manner as the lpr command.

alias   lprm   'lprm -Pprintername'

This is also the same except that you need to enter the job number from the output you received from the lpq command.

alias   lock   lockscreen

This is an abbreviation for the lockscreen command.

****

7-4 The Login File

The *.login* file is read in after the *.cshrc* file when you log into the system. You can include commands like you did for the *.cshrc* file, but you should only use the *.login* file for setting up areas such as terminal characteristics, terminal types, (when logging in over a modem), and setting environment variables. Unlike the shell variables you set up in the *.cshrc* file, environment variables are passed along to programs and shells automatically, so this file is only read once at login time.

The environment variables are what you want all programs to know about; for instance, what printer you wish to send output to, and what type of terminal you are using.

Environment variable are enabled with the "setenv" command. This command has two requirements; the name and the value.

    setenv   "name"   "value"

Environment variables are usually set with all capital letters. Although this is not mandatory, it makes it easy to separate the shell variables from the environment variables.

Now you will create a sample .login file. You may enter this file in as you see it here. At the end of the file each entry will be explained as they appear. You may also copy the generic .login file from the directory /usr/lib called Login.

    ltahoe% cp /usr/lib/Login ~/.login

As with the *.cshrc* example, please type carefuly and remember that "#" signs indicate a comment and are not read by the system.

```
###############################################
###############################################
#
#                    Sample .login file for your home directory
#
#

#                    Terminal characteristics for remote terminals:

#                    Remove the comment (#) for the terminal type
#                    you have. Leave the rest commented out for
#                    future reference.
```

```
if ($TERM != "sun") then
#eval 'tset -sQ -m dialup:?925 -m switch:?925 -m dumb:?925 $TERM'
#eval 'tset -sQ -m dialup:?h19 -m switch:?h19 -m dumb:?h19 $TERM'
#eval 'tset -sQ -m dialup:?mac -m switch:?mac -m dumb:?mac $TERM'
#eval 'tset -sQ -m dialup:?vt100 -m switch:?vt100 -m dumb:?vt100 $TERM'
#eval 'tset -sQ -m dialup:?wyse-nk -m switch:?wyse-nk -m dumb:?wyse-nk $TERM'
#eval 'tset -sQ -m dialup:?wyse-vp -m switch:?wyse-vp -m dumb:?wyse-vp $TERM'
endif

#
#                              General terminal characteristics
#

#stty -crterase
#stty -tabs
#stty crt
#stty erase 'h'
#stty werase '?'
#stty kill '['

#
#                              Environment variables
#

#setenv EXINIT 'set sh=/bin/csh sw=4 ai report=2'
#setenv MORE '-c'
#setenv PRINTER lw
setenv ROOTMENU -/.rootmenu

#       commands to perform at login

#w      # see who is logged in

if ("'tty'" != "/dev/console") exit
echo -n "SunView? (Control-C to interrupt) "
sleep 5
sunview
##########################################################
```

So let's see what all this stuff in the file actually does . . .

if ($TERM != "sun") then

This states that if you are logging in from a terminal other than a Sun workstation, then execute the commands from here to the endif. (This means to take all commands until an endif is encountered in the file)

The following lines will describe the setup for different terminal types you may be logging in on. Find the one that matches your terminal type and remove the "#" sign. If you do not see your particular terminal type, then take the first line and change the name to your terminal type. (See your system administrator if this does not work.)

#eval 'tset -sQ -m dialup:?925 -m switch:?925 -m dumb:?925 $TERM

This will set up the terminal characteristics for a Televideo 925 terminal

#eval 'tset -sQ -m dialup:?h19 -m switch:?h19 -m dumb:?h19 $TERM'

This will set up the terminal characteristics for a Heathkit H19 terminal

#eval 'tset -sQ -m dialup:?mac -m switch:?mac -m dumb:?mac $TERM'

This will set up the terminal characteristics for a Macintosh running Macterminal

#eval 'tset -sQ -m dialup:?vt100 -m switch:?vt100 -m dumb:?vt100 $TERM'

This will set up the terminal characteristics for a VT100 terminal

#eval 'tset -sQ -m dialup:?wyse-nk -m switch:?wyse-nk -m dumb:?wyse-nk $TERM'

This will set up the terminal characteristics for a Wyse-50 terminal

#eval 'tset -sQ -m dialup:?wyse-vp -m switch:?wyse-vp -m dumb:?wyse-vp $TERM'

This will set up the terminal characteristics for a Wyse 50 in ADDS viewpoint mode with "enhance" turned on

endif

This ends the terminal evaluation statement. If you had logged in from another Sun Workstation, the statement would not have been true and you would have skipped this part of the .login file.

Once you read the explanations for the next few lines, uncomment out the terminal characteristics you will want on your system.

#stty -crterase

This will set up the erase function to backspace without removing the characters until you overwrite them with new ones.

#stty -tabs

This will convert tabs to spaces when they are displayed on the screen

#stty crt

This will set up the standard crt characteristics (if you use this, you do not need the others)

#stty erase '^h'

This sets the erase function to be the Back-Space key.

#stty werase '^?'

This will set the erase-word function to be the Delete key

#stty kill '^['

This will set the kill function to be the Esc key

Environment variables

setenv   EXINIT   'set sh=/bin/csh sw=4 ai report=2'

This will set up some basic "vi" variables. There are other ways to set up the vi variables. This is with the .exrc file. (See the section on vi.) If you use the EXINIT environment variable, then the .exrc file is ignored.

setenv   MORE   '-c'

This will make the "more" command overwrite the screen rather than scroll down the page. It makes reading long files much easier.

#setenv   PRINTER   "printername"

This will tell the system which printer you will normally use. If your system administrator has set the alternate name of your printer to "lw", then that should be the default. Unless you know how the /etc/printcap file is set up, you should use the name of the printer that you already know.

setenv   ROOTMENU   ~/.rootmenu

This will force SunView to look at your home directory for the SunView menu definition file. Otherwise it will use the default menu file in /usr/lib.

> \# Commands to perform at login

This area is for your own personal commands you wish to have.

> \#w \# See who is logged in

This will tell you who is logged in as you log in yourself.

```
if (" 'tty' " != "/dev/console") exit
echo -n "SunView? (Control-C to interrupt)"
sleep 5
sunview
```

This little package will place you into SunView automatically after you log in. It will ask you if you want to stop the entry into SunView and wait 5 seconds. Then it will enter the SunView application.

7-5 The Mailrc File

Your *.mailrc* file will control the appearance and functionality of the mail and mailtool programs. The best way to build this file is from the Defaults Editor program in SunView. For the most complete description of all options available for mail and mailtool, please see the section on Defaults Editor in the editors chapter. If you wish to build a quick *.mailrc* file then stay tuned and you will go over the basic items.

You may also copy the generic *.mailrc* file from the */usr/lib* directory called Mailrc. To copy this file, enter the command:

```
ltahoe% cp /usr/lib/Mailrc  -/.mailrc

#############################################
##
##                              Sample .mailrc file
##

set alwaysignore
set askcc
set asksub
set autoprint
```

```
set DEAD=-/dead.letter
set hold
set indentprefix=">"
set keepsave
set record=-/outbox
set VISUAL=/usr/ucb/vi

ignore apparently-to date errors-to from id in-reply-to /
        message-id precedence received references
        remailed-date / remailed-from return-path sent-by
        status via
######################################################
######################################################
```

Now you will see what is set for mail and mailtool options.

When you see reference to "normally turned off", it means that if you do not set this variable, then you will not have that function.

set alwaysignore

In the last line of the .mailrc file, you have some lines that you want to be ignored. That is, you do not want to see these lines when you are viewing mail. With the alwaysignore variable set, not only will you not see these lines when you view mail, but you will not save them when you reply to mail or save a mail message to a file.

set askcc

This variable will turn on the Cc: (carbon copy) prompt when composing a letter. The default is normally off.

set asksub

When this is set you will automatically be prompted for a subject when composing a letter.

set autoprint

When you have more than one mail message to view, auto-print will display the next message automatically when you delete the previous message. This is normally turned off.

set DEAD=-/dead.letter

This is where a partial letter is stored in the event of a power failure or system crash. The path to this file is set to your home directory.

set hold

When the hold variable is turned on, all letters that you have already read are kept in the mailbox until you delete or save them. If hold is not set, then the letters are moved to a file, usually called mbox in your home directory. This is accomplished when you hit the commit button under the "done" button in mailtool.

set indentprefix=">"

Let's say you are replying to a letter and you include the original letter in your mail. What this variable does is place a ">" sign before each line of the included letter. This makes it easier to distinguish between your letter and the included letter.

set keepsave

When you save a letter to a file, the system typically removes the file from the mailbox. With keepsave turned on, the letter is saved to a file and the original will remain in your mailbox. This has the same function as the copy option in mailtool.

set record=~/outbox

This will save a copy of every mail message you send out in a file under your home directory called outbox. In this way you can bring up the file with the folder button in mailtool and review or resend a previously composed letter.

set VISUAL=/usr/ucb/vi

This is the editor you will use with the v option in mail. You may set this to any editor you choose. The default is vi.

ignore apparently-to date errors-to from id in-reply-to / message-id
precedence received references remailed-date / remailed-from
return-path sent-by status via

ignore will specify all of the information you do not wish to see when looking at mail messages. This is usually a large block of information that explains detailed aspects of the mail message.

7-6 The Sunview File

Now you will take a look at a sample .sunview file. This will be covered in greater detail in the section on SunView. This is only an overview of a sample .sunview file. You will create a new one in the chapter on SunView.

The .sunview file will tell the system what your windows will look like when running SunView. It will contain information about the size, labeling and position of each window or tool.

You may copy the generic .sunview file from the /usr/lib directory called .suntools. To copy this file, enter the command:

```
ltahoe% cp /usr/lib/.suntools   ~/.sunview
```

```
##############################################
cmdtool  -Wp   0    0 -WP     0  0 -Wh   3 -Ww 80 -Wl  "<< CONSOLE >>"-WL
                                              "console"
clock     -Wp 497   32 -WP  704  0 -Wi   -Wh  1
cmdtool  -Wp    0   71 -WP  772  0 -Wi   -Wh  44 -Ww 80
textedit  -Wp 259   98 -WP  840  0 -Wi
mailtool  -Wp 492   71 -WP  908  0 -Wi
##############################################
```

This is a basic default .sunview file for a black and white system. If you have a color system, you can create your own color scheme in SunView. This is covered in the section on SunView. Now let's look at this file and figure out what it means.

cmdtool -Wp 0 0 -WP 0 0 -Wh 3 -Ww 80 -Wl "<< CONSOLE >>" -WL "console" -C

The first line will bring up a command tool that will be used as your console window. You need this so the system has a place to send messages to. If you do not have a console window, the system will print messages in the middle of your screen. An example of system messages are talk requests from other users, shutdown messages from your system administrator, and any error massages the system may have to inform you about.

Let's decipher this mixup of letters and numbers.

The first option is -Wp, followed by 0 0. This tells the system where to place the window on the screen. The W stands for window, the p stands for position. In this case it would place the commandtool in the upper left corner of the screen. The numbers represent pixels. The first number is for the x axis and the second is for the y axis. (Don't worry if you do not understand this because the toolplaces command will set these numbers for you.)

The next option is the -WP option. This will tell the system where to place the icon when the window is closed. It uses the same attributes as -Wp does.

Now you have the -Wh option or window height. The number following the -Wh stands for the height of the window in text lines. In this case the window will be 3 lines high.

Next is -Ww. You guessed it, it's window width. This is the width of the window in columns. For this window it will be 80 columns wide.

The -Wl stands for window label. This will place a label in the top border of the open window as <<CONSOLE>>. By open window it is meant that the window is not in an iconic or closed state.

The -WL option stands for Window icon label. This will place a label in the icon. It will read "console" when the window is closed to an icon.

And last but not least is the -C option. This tells the system that this window is a console window where system messages are logged.

As for the rest of the tools you should be able to see just what is being done for each by looking at the map of arguments below. For the rest of the tools in the file you can see that the -Wi option is set. This will bring up the tools in a closed position, which means they will first appear on the screen as an icon.

An entry in this file can be for a mailtool, schedule tool, a clock or any SunView window tool that you have available to you.

Here is the man page listing of the arguments for window based tools and there explanations. Try and compare their explanations with the options you see in the sample .sunview file. It should make some sense to you now.

FLAG	(LONG FLAG)	ARGUMENTS	NOTES
-Ww	(-width)	columns	
-Wh	(-height)	lines	
-Ws	(-size)	x y	x and y are in pixels
-Wp	(-position)	x y	x and y are in pixels
-WP	(-icon__position)	x y	x and y are in pixels
-Wl	(-label)	"string"	
-Wi	(-iconic)		makes the application start iconic (closed)
-Wt	(-font)	filename	
-Wn	(-no__name__stripe)		
-Wf	(-foreground__color)	red green blue	0-255 (no color-full color)
-Wb	(-background__color)	red green blue	0-255 (no color-full color)
-Wg	(-set__default__color)		(apply color to subwindows too)
-WI	(-icon__image)	filename	(for applications with non-default icons)
-WL	(-icon__label)	"string"	(for applications with non-default icons)

| -WT | (-icon_font) | filename | (for applications with non-default icons) |
| -WH | (-help) | | print this table |

Remember, you will cover this more closely in the section on SunView. This was only to familiarize you with the .sunview file and what it represents.

7-7 The Defaults File

The .defaults file is created when you use the Defaults Editor. The Defaults Editor is a SunView tool that allows you to change the standard defaults for SunView. When you say default, you mean a standard way of using the system. To change this method you need to change its default values. You will go through the Defaults Editor in the chapter on Editors.

Here you will only see some basic .defaults entries so you can familiarize yourself with the file.

This file will represent only an example of what your .defaults will contain.

```
###########################################
SunDefaults_Version 2
/Mail/Set/interval          "5"
/Mail/Set/printmail         "\"lpr -p -h -Ppip\""
/Mail/Set/alwaysignore      "Yes"
/Mail/Set/askcc "Yes"
/Mail/Set/hold "Yes"
/Mail/Set/autoprint         "Yes"
/Mail/Set/record            "/outbox"
/Menu/Initial_Selection     "Last_Selection"
/SunView/Alert_Bell         "2"
/SunView/Embolden_Labels        "Enabled"
###########################################
```

Let's briefly describe each line. Notice that many of the defaults you see here you also set in your .mailrc file.

```
/Mail/Set/interval      "5"
```

This will set the number of seconds your system will wait before checking for mail again. You can change this to any time length you like.

```
/Mail/Set/printmail        "\"lpr -p -Ppip\""
```

Here you tell mailtool which printer to print to and which options you would like to have. In this case you are using the lpr command with the -p option and sending the mail to a printer called "pip". The -p option uses the pr program which formats the files for printing. The backlashes in the line tell the shell to ignore the next (") and not to take them literally.

/Mail/Set/alwaysignore   "Yes"

In the last line of the .mailrc file, you have some lines that you want to be ignored. That is you do not want to see these lines when you are viewing mail. With the alwaysignore variable set, not only will you not see these lines when you view mail, but you will not save them when you reply to mail or save a mail message to a file.

/Mail/Set/askcc   "Yes"

This variable will turn on the Cc: (carbon copy) prompt when composing a letter. The default is normally off.

/Mail/Set/hold   "Yes"

When the hold variable is turned on, all letters that you have already read are kept in the mailbox until you delete or save them. If hold is not set, then the letters are moved to a file, usually called mbox in your home directory. This is accomplished when you choose the commit selection under the "done" button in mailtool.

/Mail/Set/autoprint   "Yes"

When you have more than one mail message to view, autoprint will display the next message automatically when you delete the previous message. This is normally turned off.

/Mail/Set/record   "/outbox"

This will save a copy of every mail message you send out in a file under your home directory called outbox. In this way you can bring up the file with the folder button in mailtool and review or resend a previously composed letter.

/Menu/Initial_Selection "Last_Selection"

When you bring up a menu in SunView, what ever the last selection that was chosen will be the selection that is highlighted when you bring up the menu again. The default is whatever the program has as an initial selection.

/SunView/Alert__Bell   "2"

This specifies the number of times the system bell will ring when an alert message is displayed.

/SunView/Embolden__Labels   "Enabled"

This will set all tool labels to be in "bold" face.

So now you know what a basic .defaults file will look like. Once you run the Defaults Editor, you may see many entries in this file. The Defaults Editor will explain each entry when you try to make a change to the standard default. Give it a try. Play with the different settings to see which defaults you would like to change for your environment.

7-8 The Rootmenu File

The *.rootmenu* file defines what selections will appear when you bring up a menu in SunView. This is defined in greater detail in the section on SunView. As in some of the other .files you have looked at, you will only look at some basic items to give you a brief understanding of the file and its functions.

Here is the default *.rootmenu* file that comes with your system. You will first look at the first section and explain what the entries stand for. You will not go into great detail here as this will become repetitive when you read the section on SunView.

You should copy this file from */usr/lib* into your home directory. To do this enter the command:

ltahoe% **cp /usr/lib/.rootmenu** -**/.rootmenu**

Now you have a local copy that you can edit if you wish.

```
******************************************************************
#        sunview rootmenu file
#
"Shells"                            MENU
         "Command Tool"                     cmdtool
         "Shell Tool"                       shelltool
         "Graphics Tool"                    gfxtool
         "Console"                          cmdtool -C
"Shells"                            END
"Editors"                           MENU
         "Text Editor"                      textedit
         "Defaults Editor"                  defaultsedit
```

"Icon Editor"		iconedit
"Font Editor"		fontedit
"Editors"	END	
"Tools"	MENU	
"Mail Tool"		mailtool
"Dbx (debug) Tool"		dbxtool
"Performance Meter"	MENU	
"Percent CPU Used"		perfmeter -v cpu
"Ethernet Packets"		perfmeter -v pkts
"Swapped Jobs"		perfmeter -v swap
"Disk Transfers"		perfmeter -v disk
"Performance Meter"	END	
"Clock"	MENU	
</usr/include/ images/clock.icon>		clock
</usr/include/ images/ clock.rom.icon>		clock -r
"Clock"	END	
"Tools"	END	
"Services"	MENU	
"Redisplay All"	REFRESH	
"Printing"	MENU	

"Check Printer Queue" sh -c "echo; echo '----------------'; echo 'Printer queue'; lpq; echo '----------------' "

"Print Selected Text" sh -c "get_selection | lpr ; echo 'Selection printed'."

"Printing"	END	
"Remote Login"	MENU	
"Command Tool"		cmdtool csh -c "echo -n 'Hostname? '; exec

rlogin $<"

"Shell Tool"		shelltool csh -c "echo -n 'Hostname? ';

exec rlogin $<"

"Remote Login"	END	
"Save Layout"		sh -c "mv -f $HOME/.sunview

$HOME/.sunview-;toolplaces>.sunview; echo 'Screen layout saved (Previous layout in .sunview-' "

"Lock Screen"		lockscreen
"Services"	END	
"Exit SunView"	EXIT	

###

You're probably saying to yourself "What a mess, I think I will skip this part and go on to another section."

It's not as bad as you think. First you need to understand what a menu does for you. Then this file will make more sense.

As stated before, the *.rootmenu* file will display tools and services that you will use frequently in SunView. For instance, if you use lockscreen regularly, you will not want to type the command lockscreen all of the time. With a menu, you can call up the lockscreen command with the mouse. By clicking on the lockscreen option, the lockscreen command will be executed and you would not have had to type a thing.

But how does the lockscreen command become an option? This is what the *.rootmenu* file does for us. It allows you to choose what you want as mouse selectable options in SunView.

Now let's see what the first part of the file does.

```
"Shells"                    MENU
        "Command Tool"          cmdtool
        "Shell Tool"            shelltool
        "Graphics Tool"         gfxtool
        "Console"               cmdtool -C
"Shells"                    END
```

The first entry in this file specifies the title of the menu item. It is always placed within quotes (" "). This is followed by, in this case, the name of a sub-menu specified by the MENU entry. Whenever the MENU entry is there, there will be a sub-menu after it. You will normally see this referred to as "Pull-Right" menus. Any items placed in (" ") means that it is the name that will appear in the menu window. After the MENU entry is the name of the options in the sub-menu. The first entry is "Command Tool", then the actual command itself. If you look at the rootmenu by holding down the right mouse button in a gray area of the screen, you will see the initial SHELLS title, and an arrow next to it. By dragging the mouse to the right while continuing to hold the right mouse button you will enter a new menu, or "sub-menu". This will contain the new menu options which will point to the actual command. The "END" means that this is the end of the sub-menu definitions.

By now you should at least have a basic understanding of what this file is about. In the section on SunView, you will describe how to edit this file and add your own menu options.

SunView

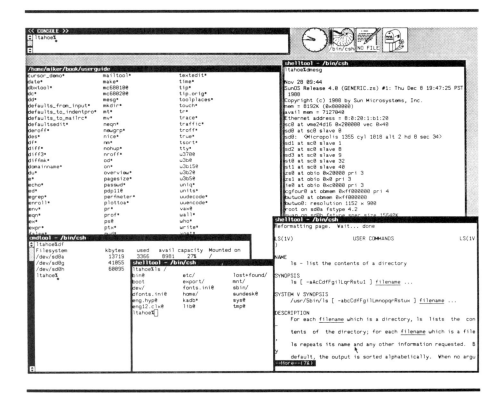

FIGURE 8.1. *A typical SunView screen layout.*

8-1 Starting SunView

Here you are at the nitty gritty of the Sun system. You will find that
SunView is the center of your working environment; virtually
everything that you do will be from SunView. It's critical for you to
discover what SunView is all about.

SunView is a window system where you can have multiple
windows or "frames" displayed at one time. This means you can

look at the contents of several directories, execute commands, and log into other systems, all at the same time. Windows or frames can be placed anywhere on the screen. They can be moved, re-sized and closed into an icon for future use.

Begin by starting up a SunView application. Move into your home directory by typing the command "**cd**" from the prompt:

```
ltahoe% cd
```

To start the SunView application, enter "sunview" on the command line.

```
ltahoe% sunview
```

8-2 Basic SunView Screen

You will see your screen go blank and turn gray. This gray area is the background of SunView. Soon all of the pre-defined tools begin to appear. If you read Chapter 7 on your home directory, you will have an understanding of what the system is doing right now. Basically, it is reading in the .sunview file from your home directory. If you do not have this file in your home directory it will be reading the default .sunview file located under */usr/lib*. Let's assume that you do not have a local **.sunview** file and are reading the default file.

Several items have now been displayed on the screen. (See Figure 8.2.)

Here is the order of appearance of tools from the default .sunview file:

*   An open console window
*   A Clock icon (round face clock)
*   A Command Tool icon (a shell with a scrollbar)
*   A Text Editor icon (a letter with a pencil)
*   A Mail Tool icon (a mailbox)

All of these items are frames which are associated with a specific tool or application. The console frame is in an "open" state, the others are in a "closed" or iconic state. When a frame is open, it can receive commands through the keyboard and mouse. Now let's define open and closed a little better. Figure 8.3 is the screen for an open Command Tool.

An example of a SunView command closed to an icon is shown in Figure 8.4.

FIGURE 8.2. *The default SunView screen.*

When you close a window you are changing the window so it does not take up room on the screen and can be called back at a later time. If a process is running in a window and you close the window to iconic, the process will continue to run. Think of closing a window as putting it away for a while until it finishes whatever it is you had it doing, or just tidying up your screen for now.

The first item to appear was the console window. This is a command tool (Identifiable by the scroll bar on the left side of the window). The console window is in an open state because this is where the system error messages are displayed. If the console window is closed, you will miss an important message from the system about the network or other system problems. The console window should always be left open somewhere on the screen. It

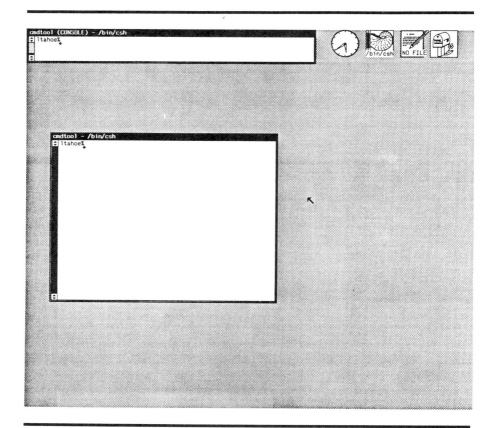

FIGURE 8.3.   *The SunView command tool.*

can be identified by the << CONSOLE >> label in the upper
border of the window.

The other items are all closed frames. The clock is a standard
clock. There are options to this clock which can make it square or
with Roman numerals. Refer to the manual page on clock for further instructions. You can also select the clock options from the
SunView main menu.

The next item is a closed Command Tool. This is the shell
with a scroll bar on the left. The command tool allows you to scroll
backwards and forwards in the window, as well as execute commands. It also has special text editing features.

Next you have a Text Editor Icon. This is a tool which is used
for advanced editing of text (See Chapter 6 on Editors, for a description of the Text Editor.)

FIGURE 8.4. *The SunView command tool which has been closed to an icon.*

Last is the Mailtool icon. This icon has a picture of a mailbox and a flag. When the flag is up, there is mail for you, and you will also see a small letter in the mail slot if you look close enough.

Now you have seen all of the default tools that appear when you invoke **sunview**. So let's do something in SunView and see this fancy stuff in action.

8-3 Using the Mouse

You know what a tool looks like in an iconic state, but how do you open these windows? To do this you should look first at how to use the mouse. The mouse is like a pilot to SunView. It allows you to select, open, and close windows, as well as manipulate and select menus, menu items and text.

Look on the screen and locate a black arrow pointing north-west. This is the pointer. It is used to select the window you wish to work in as well as the others that were mentioned. The mouse has three buttons which are used to select different actions. The mouse button definitions are as follows:

Left Button-   Referenced as "left", is used to open icons, push panel buttons, and to select text.

Middle Button-   Referenced as "middle", is used to move frames or icons, scroll in a window, and to complete text selections.

Right Button-   Referenced as "right", is used to select and choose items from menus.

Note: Left handed "mousing". If you are left handed you can change your keyboard and mouse so that its layout is reversed. You can do this by using the Defaults Editor and selecting the Left — Handed option under the input category. (See the section on the Defaults Editor.)

The mouse should be positioned with the cord (or tail) away from you and the three buttons resting under your fingertips. The mouse pad should have the wide edge facing you.

There are two ways to make selections with the mouse. There is the click selection, and the hold selection. When you are asked to click on a button, depress the requested button and release it. If you are asked to hold a button, depress the requested button and hold it down. Clicking will execute a specific selection, while holding will allow you to manipulate menu selections, or move and re-size windows. It will be easier if you just go ahead and do something with the mouse.

Now try opening an icon in the upper part of the screen. Move the mouse and watch the arrow move around the screen. Now move the arrow over the icon with the shell on it. Click left while over the icon. The icon has now changed to a Command Tool window. This window is now ready to receive commands as it is now in the open state.

Now that you have opened a window with the mouse, you will need to use the other mouse buttons to allow you to get comfortable with them. Try moving the pointer onto the upper border in the right corner of the Command Tool that you just opened. Using the top border is best as it is wider and easier to position the arrow. Notice that the arrow has now turned into a target, (a circle with a dot in the middle) now you can move or re-size the window. For now, only try to move the window as you have not worked with menus yet. With the arrow (now a target) over the top border, hold the middle mouse button down and "drag" the mouse to the right of the screen. Notice the basic window stays put while an image of a border moves with the mouse. Place the image where you would like the window to go and release the mouse button. The window will now relocate itself to the new location. If you place the arrow over the middle of a border, the window will only move up and down, or left to right. If you place the arrow near a corner, the window can be moved diagonally as well.

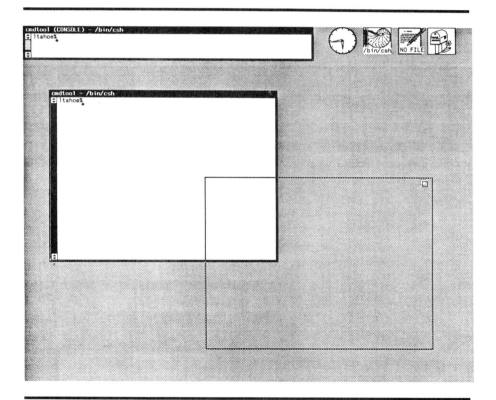

FIGURE 8.5. *Example of moving a window with the mouse.*

The right mouse button is used for menu selections. For now just so you can see what a menu looks like, move the arrow into the gray area of the screen and hold the right mouse button down. You will see the main sunview menu appear. Don't do anything with the arrow at this time as you will talk about how to use menus next. Release the button and the menu will disappear.

8-4 Menus

Menus are what you use to select options and tools in SunView. There are many types of menus which select items such as tools, services, and text aids. You had a glimpse of the main SunView menu a minute ago. Let's go back to that menu and try a few selections.

Bring up the main SunView menu again by holding the right mouse button down in a gray area of the screen. The menu will appear to the right of the arrow.

The SunView main menu is defined in a file called ".root-menu". There is a default .rootmenu file located under */usr/lib*.

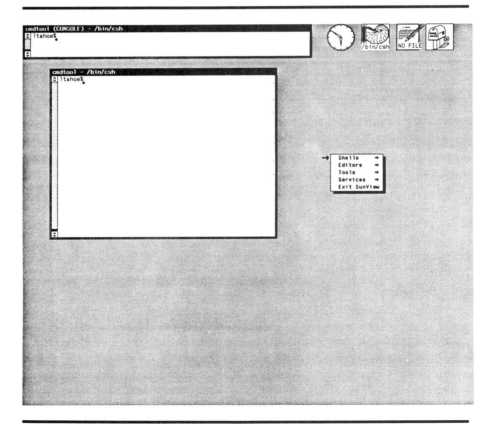

FIGURE 8.6. *Main SunView menu.*

You can customize this menu to suit your needs. In the chapter on Home Directory, you made a copy of this file and placed it in your home directory. If you did not do so yet, please copy it over now. To do this enter the command:

ltahoe% **cp /usr/lib/.rootmenu ~**

Now you have a copy you can edit for yourself, rather than editing the system's generic *.rootmenu* file.

If you look at the menu there are several selections to choose from. All but the last have an arrow to the right of the selection. This means that there are Pull-Right or sub-menus that will give you more options to select. While holding the right button down, move the arrow over the selection named "shells". Notice the label has turned black. You have now selected the shells menu. Continue to move the mouse to the right and a new menu will appear.

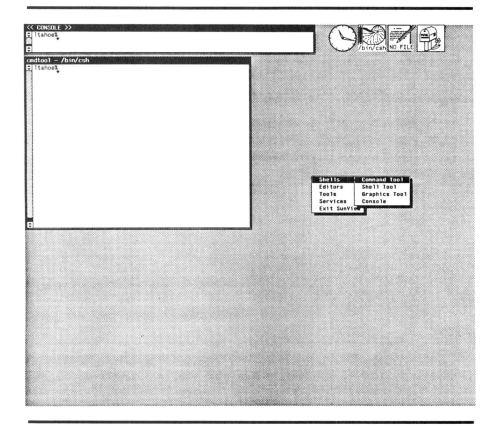

FIGURE 8.7. *Main SunView menu with selected sub-menu.*

This menu has the selections for all the different shells you may choose from. (REMEMBER TO KEEP HOLDING THE BUTTON DOWN WHILE MAKING SELECTIONS.) If you move the mouse down you can highlight the different tools. Highlight the selection marked "commandtool", then release the right mouse button. You have just asked the system to bring up a new commandtool window. The new window should appear on the screen. Try bringing up a shelltool on your own. (Note: Do not have more than one mailtool or console window on your screen at a time as you only want one each of these.)

By now you have three windows open on your screen. Let's get rid of a couple by bringing up a "frame menu".

Frame Menus

In the last example you looked at the main SunView menu. Now you will look at a frame menu. The frame menu is one way you can close, re-size, relocate and quit a frame or window. To bring up a frame menu, move the arrow over the border of a window. It should change to a target. Then hold the right mouse button down. A frame menu should appear. (See Figure 8.8.)

Here you have several selections for manipulating frames. While pressing the right mouse button, highlight the "quit" selection on the menu, then release the mouse button. You should now see a small conformation window appear asking you if you are sure you want to quit the process. Click left on the confirm button and the window will disappear. If you would have selected cancel, the window will stay up and the small conformation window will disappear.

Gray Menu Items

The gray menu selections that you see, like props in the frame menu, are for future releases and are not available at this time. If you try to select a gray selection, nothing will happen.

8-5 Re-sizing Windows

You can bring up a window now, and get rid of it. The next step is to see how you can re-size and position your windows where you want them. In the previous lesson you learned about moving win-

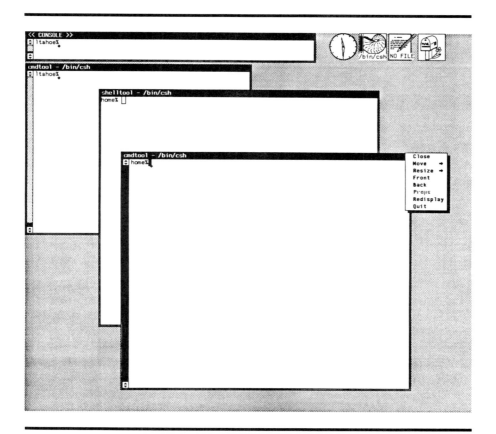

FIGURE 8.8. *SunView window frame menu.*

dows with the middle mouse button. You can also re-size the
window with this button. You may have noticed in the frame menu
a selection titled "re-size". You can change the size of the window
in this manner by highlighting the unconstrained selection in
the re-size sub-menu. Unconstrained means that you can change
the shape of the window height "and" width at the same time.
If you were to choose constrained, you could only change the
height "or" the width, depending on which border you place the
arrow on.

Try to re-size a window using the menu method. Click right
on any border of any window and select the re-size option, then
move to the right and in the sub-menu select unconstrained. A
small information window will appear telling you to place the

curser on a border while holding the right mouse button down and dragging the mouse to reshape the window to your liking. Once you have the window sized, release the right mouse button and the window will change its shape to the size you selected.

Fast Re-Sizing

There is a much faster way to re-size a window. You can re-size a window by using the middle mouse button and the control key together. Move the arrow onto a window border near a corner. The pointer should change to a target. Now hold down the control key and the middle mouse button at the same time. You should see the frame image appear. Resize the window to your liking and release the middle button and the control key and the window will now be re-sized. Remember as before, if you move the pointer to the middle of a border, you can only re-size in one direction. If you have the pointer near a corner, you can re-size in both directions.

8-6 Positioning Windows

You now know how to re-size the window, so place them in different locations. As with resizing windows, positioning them works in the same fashion. Let's bring up the frame menu again and highlight the "move" option in the menu and bring up the move submenu. Highlight the unconstrained option and release the middle mouse button. You will see the same information window that appeared when you did the re-size. Place the pointer in the border near a corner and hold the middle mouse button down while dragging the window around in the screen. Once you have the window placed where you like, release the mouse button and the window will now be moved to the new location.

Faster Positioning

As with re-size, there is a faster way to move a window. Move the pointer over a border near a corner. Now hold down the middle mouse button and drag the window to its new location. Once the window is placed, release the mouse button and the window will be in its new position.

8-7 Exposing Hidden Windows

When you have several windows open on the screen, some of them will be overlapped or partially hidden from view. How do you move these windows to the front of other windows? Toggling between windows can be done in the same manner as moving and resizing. You can use the menu method, the mouse method, or a function key.

Exposing Hidden Windows— Menu Method

To use the menu method, find a window you wish to be in front and place the pointer on any border of the window. Bring up the frame menu and select the front option in the menu. When you release the middle mouse button the window will now be in front of the other windows. This works the same way to hide a window. Select the back option from the menu and release the mouse button. The window will now be in back of the others.

Exposing Hidden Windows— Mouse Method

The mouse method is very simple. Select a window that you wish to have in front. Move the pointer over the window border and click the left mouse button. The window that was in the back is now in the front. The mouse method will not hide a window, only bring it to the front.

Exposing Hidden Windows—Function Key

One other method is to use the left function keys. These are the keys labeled L1 through L10 on the left side of the keyboard. You will learn these keys later, but for now you will see the L5 key. The L5 keys function is identified as front. You can use this key to toggle a window between front and back. Move the pointer into any window, hit the L5 key and the window will move either to the front or to the back depending on where it was at the time. This is by far the fastest way to toggle a window because you do not have to position the pointer on a border, anywhere in the window will work.

8-8 Moving Icons

You know how to position a window with different methods of menu and mouse. You can also position an icon to be anywhere on the screen. Treat an icon the same as you would a window. The middle mouse button is the fastest way to move an icon. Remember how you did this for windows. Test yourself and reposition the clock icon somewhere else on the screen.

Note: You cannot re-size an icon. You will see a re-size menu option in the frame menu, but it does not do anything.

Summary of Basic SunView

So far you have learned the following about SunView:

- Invoking SunView
- Opening icons
- Moving icons
- Basic menus
- Bringing up windows
- Resizing windows
- Positioning windows
- Toggling windows

With this you now have a basic understanding of how to get around in SunView. You have found by now that it is not as difficult as you thought it would be. Most of the applications in SunView are self-explanatory once you know how to use the basic tools. Try to use some of the other options to the frame menu on your own. They are just as easy as the rest were. Practice with the basics for a while until you feel comfortable in SunView.

8-9 Using Tools and Services—The SunView Menu

You are now ready to look at some of the available tools and services in SunView. From a user's point of view you will look at the ones you will use the most. There are some tools that you may never use (such as the Font Editor) that you will not cover in this book. Start by learning the generic tools and services offered in the main SunView menu.

Here is a picture of the sunview main menu

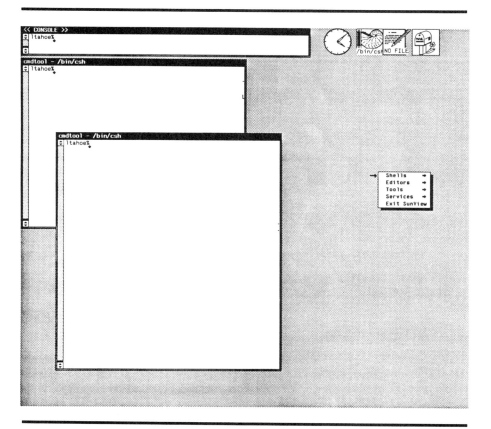

FIGURE 8.9. *SunView main menu.*

Now you will see what is below each sub-menu. You will examine each individually in a moment. When you see this symbol "=>", it means there is a sub-menu beneath this menu. They are referred to as "Pull Right" menus. Remember that to look at a Pull Right menu you must move the mouse to the right while holding down the right mouse button.

Shells=>

        Command Tool
        Shell Tool
        Graphics Tool
        Console

Editors=>

        Text Editor
        Defaults Editor
        Icon Editor
        Font Editor

Tools=>

        Mail Tool
        Dbx Tool
        Performance Meter
        Clock=>Show two icons of different clock faces.

Services=>

        Redisplay All
        Printing=>   Check Printer Queue
                           Print Selected Text
        Remote Login=>   Command Tool
                           Shell Tool

        Save Layout
        Lockscreen

Exit SunView

These are the main menu selections you have available to you. Let's look at each one and see what they do.

Shells

Command Tool	This will bring up a command tool window. This window can be used to enter system commands, scroll up and down, and also has special text editing functions.
Shell Tool	This will bring up a standard tty window. You can enter system commands in a shell tool.
Graphics Tool	This will bring up a split screen window. The upper portion will allow you to enter a command for a graphics program and observe its display in the lower portion.
Console	This will bring up a console window.

Editors

Text Editor	This will bring up a text editor window. See the section on Text Editor.
Defaults Editor	This will bring up the defaults editor window. This is used to change the system defaults. See the section on defaults editor.

Icon Editor	This will bring up an icon editor window. This tool allows you to create your own icons. See the section on icon editor.
Font Editor	This will bring up a font editing window. this is used to create your own font sets. Not covered in this book. See the Sun Reference Manual.

Tools

Mail Tool	This is the system mail window. This tool allows you to compose and view e-mail. See the section on e-mail.
Dbx Tool	This is a debugging tool for the source code of C, Pascal, and Fortran programs.
Performance Meter	These are used to monitor system performance. You have a choice of cpu usage, Ethernet packets, swapped jobs, and disk transfers.
Clock=>	Here you have a choice of a round clock or a square clock with Roman numerals. These are shown in iconic form.

Services

Redisplay All	This will redisplay the screen in the event of garbage on the screen.
Printing	Here you have two options. You can examine the printer queue, or you can print any text you have selected.
Remote Login=>	This gives you a sub-menu with a choice of a commandtool or a shelltool. Here the system will bring up the selected tool and ask you for a hostname of the system you wish to log into.
Save Layout	This will create a .sunview file using the current screen layout. If you already have a current .sunview file, it will rename it *.sunview-* and then write the new file. (See the section on the *.sunview* file.)
Lockscreen	This will produce a constantly moving pattern using a Sun logo which will cover the entire screen. This prevents the screen from being "burned" as well as keeping others from using your system when you are not using it. Screen burn is when the same image stays on the screen for long periods of time. Eventually the image will burn the phosphor on the screen and you will see faint images of things that are not

| | there. To exit lockscreen, press any key and enter your password. |
| Exit SunView | This will exit the SunView application and place you back in the initial login shell. |

8-10 Adding Menu Items

Now you have an understanding of the SunView main menu. You saw earlier that this menu is defined by the *.rootmenu* file. Now try adding an additional menu item. Say you like to play backgammon and will be using the game "gammontool" located in /usr/games. You can add this tool to the meny by editing the *.rootmenu* file in your home directory and adding the following:

    "Gammontool"   /usr/games/gammontool

Here is how it would look like placed at the bottom of the .rootmenu file.

"Lock Screen"	lockscreen
"Services"	END
"Exit SunView"	EXIT
"Gammontool"	/usr/games/gammontool

For each item you would like to see in a menu, specify the name of the item in quotes, then the actual command that you want to execute. There can be no blank lines in this file. You can have comments which start with a #, but do not leave any lines empty. Figure 8-10 shows how your menu will now appear with the new Gammontool entry.

Adding Pull-Right Menu Items

For menu items with Pull-Right menus, "=>", you need to specify the menu title followed by MENU, and ended with END. Here is an example of making a Pull-Right menu selection.

Let's replace your last example. You had a menu selection for Gammontool. Why not change this heading to "Games" and have a Pull-Right menu selection for gammontool and chesstool. To do this you will add the following to the bottom of your *.rootmenu* file. (Delete the gammontool entry.)

| "Lock Screen" | lockscreen |
| "Services" | END |

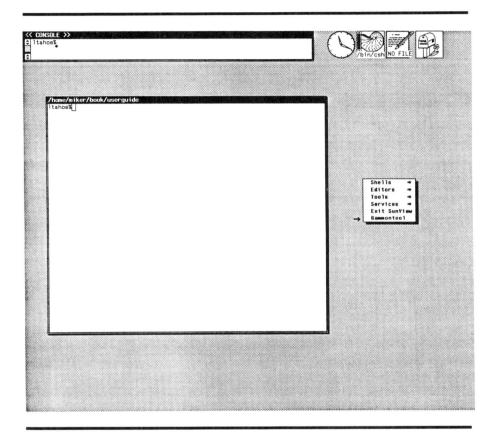

FIGURE 8.10. *Sunview main menu with additional menu entry.*

"Exit SunView"	EXIT
"Games"	MENU
"Gammontool"	/usr/games/gammontool
"Chesstool"	/usr/games/chesstool
"Games"	END

You can now look at your new SunView menu and it will have the new selections available. (See Figure 8.11.)

Remember: You must have the ROOTMENU environment variable set in your *.login* file, or the entry in the defaults editor set to your home directory's *.rootmenu* file. (See Chapter 6 on Editors for information on the Defaults Editor.)

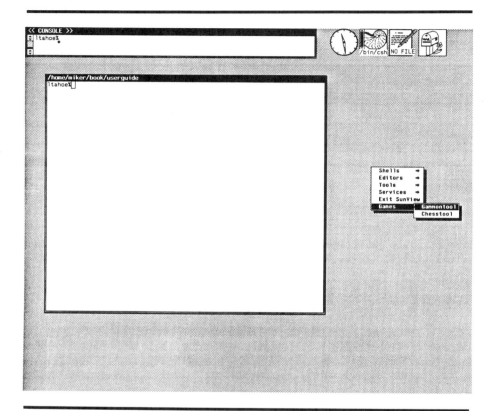

FIGURE 8.11. *Adding pull-right menu selections. New pull-right menu selection.*

8-11 Using Icons in the SunView Menu

If you looked at the clock menu items you noticed that instead of a name selection, an icon was displayed. You can have icons as menu selections in SunView. Say you want to change the games entries for gammontool and chesstool to the actual icons that the tools have. All you have to do is change the menu item name from gammontool to the name of the icon. All standard system icons are located in the directory */usr/include/images*. They are the files that end in .icon. For gammontool and chesstool, the icon file names are gammon.icon and chesstool.icon. Replace the menu selections for gammontool and chesstool with these filenames enclosed in brackets "<>". You must include the full path to the icons. To change the games menu listings to icons, edit your .root-menu file and make the following changes:

CHANGE FROM:

"Games"		MENU
	"Gammontool"	/usr/games/gammontool
	"Chesstool"	/usr/games/chesstool
"Games"		END

TO THIS:

"Games"	MENU
</usr/include/images/gammon.icon>	/usr/games/gammontool
</usr/include/images/chesstool.icon>	/usr/games/chesstool
"Games"	END

You will now see the game icons instead of the game names.

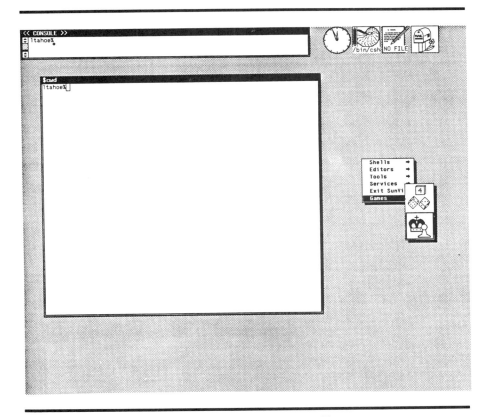

FIGURE 8.12. *SunView menu selection with icons as selectable items.*

8-12 Editing the *.sunview* File

You have seen how to make changes to the rootmenu file which tells the system how the menus will appear. But how does the system define how SunView itself appears? This is the job of the .sunview file in your home directory. If you read Chapter 7 on your home directory, you learned about this file and what resides within. The *.sunview* file is read when you invoke SunView. It contains information about what tools you will bring up, where they will be located and (for color systems), what color the windows will be. If the system cannot find a .sunview file in your home directory, it will use the default *.sunview* file located under */usr/lib*. If you have not done so already, copy this file to your home directory with the following command:

        ltahoe% **CP/usr/lib/.sunview ~**

Let's look at the default *.sunview* file.

        ltahoe% **more ~/.sunview**

```
#
#     @(#)suntools      10.12      88/02/08      SMI
#
#     default       .suntools file
#
cmdtool   -Wp     0    0 -WP    0  0 -Wh   3 - Ww 80  -Wl
                                           "<<CONSOLE>>" -WL"console"
clock     -Wp   497   32 -WP  704  0 -Wi   -Wh 1
cmdtool   -Wp     0   71 -WP  772  0 -Wi   -Wh 44  -Ww 80
textedit  -Wp   259   98 -WP  840  0 -Wi
mailtool  -Wp   492   71 -WP  908  0 -Wi
```

This is how SunView is told which tools to bring up and where to locate them. In the section on your home directory, you learned the meaning of each of these lines. You should know how to re-size windows and move them around on the screen. Take a few moments and position windows and icons where you would like to have them come up each time you enter SunView. You may want to change the clock to a square one, open several shelltools, and re-size them to the shape you like best. Once you have done this you are going to save this setup to the *.sunview* file.

Are you ready to make the save?

As noted in the section on the SunView menu, there was a

selection under "Services" called "'Save Layout". This selection will save the current screen layout and write the contents to the *.sunview* file. Go ahead and select the "Save Layout" option from the SunView menu.

Now exit SunView with the "Exit SunView" option in the SunView menu.

Go back into SunView by entering the command "sunview".

```
ltahoe% sunview
```

You should now see the same layout you had when you exited SunView.

Multiple *.sunview* Files

You now have a current screen arrangement that is usable. But what if you would like a different arrangement for doing different jobs? You can save screen layouts and rename them to the job you will be doing. For example, if you take your current *.sunview* file and rename it *.sunview_daily*, you can now create a new screen layout and save it using the "Save Layout" menu option. This will create a new *.sunview* file which you could rename to *.sunview. editing*. You now have two different files containing screen layouts for SunView. To bring up a particular screen layout, you will use the "-s" option to SunView. This option will use the specified file instead of the regular *.sunview* file.

Try moving your existing *.sunview* file to .sunview_1. The command for this would be:

```
ltahoe% mv  .sunview  .sunview_1
```

Reposition some windows and use the "Save Layout" menu option and save the current screen layout.You should now have two different screen files, one called *.sunview*, and one called *.sunview_1*. If you were to exit and re-enter SunView, your screen would have the new layout you just created. If you exit and re-enter SunView only this time specifying the old arrangement with the "-s" option and the file name, you would see your old screen layout appear.

Here is the command to specify a different screen file.

```
ltahoe% sunview  -s  .sunview_1
```

8-13 Color SunView Windows

If your system is equipped with a color monitor you can have your screen and windows appear in color. This is done by editing the *.sunview* file and adding the color scheme you wish on the line with the specific tool or application.

Color windows are defined with "foreground" and "background" colors. The background color would be the window area itself. The foreground color would be the border of the window and the text.

Colors are defined by a combination of the three color guns in the monitor. The color of these guns are red, green, and blue. As with a television, colors are generated by different intensities of the three guns. For instance, purple is a mixture of red and blue. The intensity of red and blue determines what shade of purple you will get. These intensities are defined in ranges of 0 to 255. In the *.sunview* file, you have lines which define the toolname, its location and other information. It is here that you will give it the color you want. Look at the line in the *.sunview* file which brings up the clock.

```
clock    -Wp    497    32    -WP    704    0 -Wi    -Wh 1
```

What you will do is add the color arguments to this line. The color arguments are specified with the -Wf (window foreground) and -Wb (window background).

The color ranges are listed for foreground and background in the order of red, green, and blue. So for a solid blue color, it would read as:

```
Red     Green     Blue
 0        0        255
```

You have just specified no red, no green and all blue. By adjusting these numbers you can change the color to be anything you wish. Now you will change your clock to be blue with tan numbers. The new .sunview entry for the clock would be:

```
clock  -Wp 497 32 -WP 704 0 -Wi -Wh 1 -Wf 255 208 64 -Wb 102 0 255 -Wg
```

You added -Wf 255 208 64 -Wb 102 0 255 -Wg to the clock line.

- Wf for window foreground, colors are 255 208 64

- Wb for window background, colors are 102 0 255

- Wg This will apply the colors to sub-windows as well.

Now if you re-enter Sunview, your clock will have the new color scheme that you have selected. Try editing some other tools and add the colors you wish. You do not have to exit SunView each time you change a tool color. You can cut and paste the entry from the file onto a command line and press return. This will bring up the new window. If you want the window to stay up without losing the window you entered the command in, you must run the command in the background. This is done with the "**&**" sign at the end of the command.

ltahoe% clock   -Wp 497   32 -Wp   704   0 -Wi -Wh 1 -Wf 255
208 64 -Wb 102 0 255 -Wg &

Note: One continuous line.
Here are some examples of window foreground and background colors.

Colors:

light blue	-	0	235	255
baby blue	-	0	188	255
royal blue	-	96	110	255
yellow	-	252	255	0
tan	-	255	213	0
orange	-	155	192	0
dark red	-	173	108	108
dark brown	-	173	147	22
pink	-	255	160	240
light purple	-	196	0	155
black	-	0	0	0
white	-	255	255	255

As you can see the list could be endless. Here are some pre-defined window foreground and background colors that look pretty good together.

Black background with a light blue foreground:
-Wf 0 235 255 -Wb 0 0 0 -Wg
Light blue background with a yellow foreground:
-Wf 255 255 160 -Wb 0 235 255 -Wg
Brown background with a white foreground:
-Wf 255 255 255 -Wb 214 178 0 -Wg
Vivid blue background with a white foreground:
-Wf 255 255 255 -Wb 96 110 255 -Wg
Gray background with dark blue foreground:
-Wf 0 0 200 -Wb 235 235 235 -Wg

Simply add these extensions to a .sunview file selection and you will have color!

Here is a complete *.sunview* which is set up for color. You can copy this for your own and change the colors as you like.

Note: Since the lines are longer than the regular window size, they will wrap to the next line. Be sure that each line is continuous. This means no carriage return within a line.

SAMPLE COLOR .sunview FILE:
```
***************************************************************************
#
#                           Color .sunview file
#
cmdtool      -Wp      0    0 -Ws 673  71 -WP      0    0 -Wb 200 200 200 -Wf      0
0 200 -Wl    "<< CONSOLE >>" -WL console -C -Wg
shelltool    -Wp      0   71 -Ws 650 567 -WP     64    0 -Wb 235 235 235 -Wf      0
0 200 -Wg
shelltool    -Wp    502  333 -Ws 650 567 -WP    128    0 -Wb 214 178    0 -Wf    245
245 245   -Wg
mailtool     -Wp    492   71 -Ws 670 770 -WP   1056    0 -Wi -Wb    0 214 255    -Wf
255 255 255  -Wg
textedit     -Wp    259   98 -Ws 673 764 -WP    968    0 -Wi -Wb    0 188 255    -Wf
255 255 160  -Wg
cmdtool      -Wp      0   71 -Ws 673 727 -Wp    868    0 -Wi -Wb 160 169 255    -Wf
255 235 192  -Wg
clock        -Wp    497   32 -Ws 210  47 -WP    776    0 -Wi -Wb 192 251 255    -Wf
50  132  123  -r  -Wg
***************************************************************************
```

8-14 Adding a Background in SunView

You can change the background of the SunView screen to display an image or picture. These images can be created with screen-dump or Icon Edit. Your company may already have images somewhere on a file server. Check with your system administrator to see what you have available. To bring up a raster image in the background of SunView, enter the command:

`ltahoe% sunview -background (filename)`

The filename being the raster image file. Here is picture of a foxsquirrel which is a raster image. To bring up this image you would enter the command:

```
ltahoe% sunview -background foxsquirrel .image
```

FIGURE 8.13. *SunView with a background raster image.*

Using Reverse Video

If you do not like the white background with black borders and text, you can bring up SunView in reverse video. That is a black background with white letters and border. Some users find this easier on their eyes. To do this, enter SunView with the "-i" option.

```
ltahoe% sunview -i
```

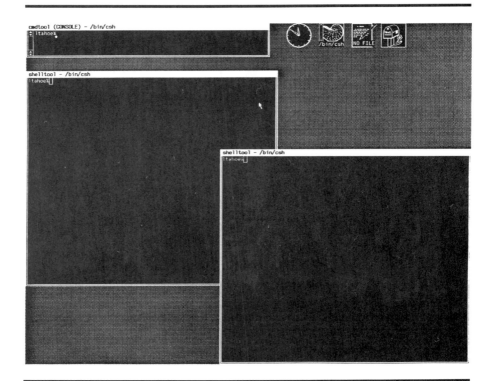

FIGURE 8.14. *SunView screen in reverse video.*

8-15 Changing the Font Size for SunView

The text size in SunView can be changed by altering the font size. This can be accomplished two different ways. One way is to change the default font setting with the Defaults Editor (see the section on Defaults Editor) or you can add the -Wt option in the description line in your .sunview file.

Here is a sample line of a shelltool in the .sunview file.

```
shelltool  -Wp  420  319  -Ws  650  567  -WP  128  0-Wi
```

Say you want the shelltool to have large text because your eyes are not what they used to be. To increase the size of this particular window, you would add the -Wt option to the end of the line, followed by the path to the font you wish to use. For instance, in this example you will use a 16 point font. This is a fairly large font.

The different types of fonts are located in the directory called
/usr/lib/fonts/fixedwidthfonts. Here you will find a variety of fonts
to choose from. You will use the cour.b.16 for this shelltool. So, by
adding:

-Wt /usr/lib/fonts/fixedwidthfonts/cour.b.16

to your existing line, you will now get a shelltool with a 16 point
font.

shelltool -Wp 420 319 -Ws 650 567 -WP 128 0
-Wi -Wt /usr/lib/fonts/fixedwidthfonts/cour.b.16

Note: The line is continuous and is not two separate lines.

You may change all of your windows to have different font
sizes, or you can specify a specific font size from the Defaults
Editor.

In Figure 8-15 is an example of a shelltool with a font size
of 24.

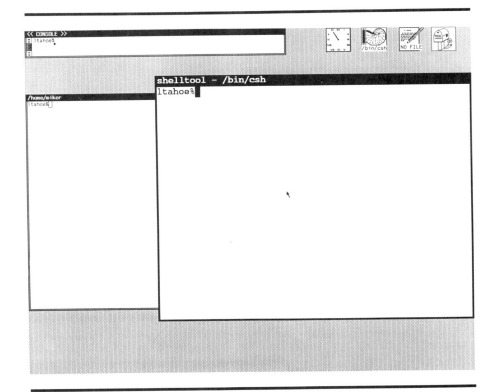

FIGURE 8.15. *Shelltool using large fonts.*

The command used to bring up this shelltool was:

ltahoe% **shelltool -Wt /usr/lib/fonts/fixedwidthfonts/cour.b.24**

Note: If you have a default font size specified from the Defaults Editor, and you specify another font size in the *.sunview* file, the font specified in the *.sunview* file will take presidence.

8-16 Running Multiple Desktops

It is possible on some Sun workstations to run multiple SunView environments on the same screen. Certain Sun systems, such as the 3/110 and 4/110, can run a SunView environment in the color plane as well as in the black and white plane. When multiple SunView processes are running you can switch between these desktops with a program called "**switcher**".

Let's start by getting into SunView in the color plane only. To do this enter this command after you have logged into the system.

ltahoe% **sunview -8bit_color_only -toggle _enable**

The system will now enter SunView but limited to only the color plane group.

Once you are in SunView, from a shelltool, enter the command:

ltahoe% **sunview -d /dev/bwtwo0 -toggle_enable &**

This will start another SunView process in the black & white plane group.

Now you need to get to the other SunView process. To do this you will use an application called "**switcher**".

From the same shelltool you started the other SunView process, enter the command:

ltahoe% **switcher -d /dev/bwtwo0 &**

You will see an icon appear that has arrows pointing in both directions. You will use this to switch between the two desktops.

To switch between desktops, either click left on the icon, or if you want to see the switch animated, select with the right mouse button and pick one of the options for switching to the other screen.

Once in the other SunView, you will need to start another switcher to get you back to the other SunView desktop. In a shelltool window, enter the command:

ltahoe% **switcher -d /dev/fb &**

This will be the switcher to get you to the color desktop. Use this switcher just like the other one.

Possible Problems Starting Multiple Desktops

You may run into a problem starting the other SunView process. This would be if the device */dev/bwtwo0* does not exist in the */dev* directory. To create this, cd into the */dev* directory, become the superuser, and execute the following command:

ltahoe# **MAKEDEV bwtwo0**

This will create the device necessary to run in the black & white plane group. You will also need to make sure that */dev/f b* exists. If it does not, create this device also.

8-17 Exiting a Stuck SunView

Once in a great while, you may experience a mouse which has decided to roll over and die. This can happen if a process in SunView gets stuck or an application does not exit gracefully. When this happens you will find out that without the mouse, you cannot exit SunView. To exit SunView when your mouse has died, follow these steps and you will be ok.

1. First find out where your mouse pointer currently is. You need the pointer to be in the grey area of the screen. If the pointer is within a window, you must close the window first. Press the L7 key, located on the left side of the keyboard. This will close the window to an icon.

2. The pointer should now be in a gray area of the screen. Now execute the following key sequence to exit SunView.

Ctrl D   then Ctrl Q   (the d and q do not have to be capitalized)

3. You should now have exited SunView.

8-18 Creating More Window Devices

SunView uses window devices to create the images you see on the screen. For instance Mail Tool uses many window devices when looking at and composing a mail message. Your system comes configured with 64 window devices located in a directory called /**dev.** When you run many SunView applications, you may run out of available window devices. But have no fear, you can increase the number of window devices on your system. To accomplish this, you need to cd into the /**dev** directory and become the super-user.

If you look at the number of window devices in /**dev,** do this by listing the contents of the /**dev** directory. You will see many devices which are named "win" with a number after it. For instance win10, win11, win12, win13 up to win63. What you want to do is increase the current number of window devices from 64 to 128. This is done with the MAKEDEV command.

The window devices are created by running MAKEDEV on a window device group. Window devices are generated in groups of 32. The window device groups are win0, win1, win2, and win3. The first group of 32 windows are win0, the second group of 32 is win1. These two window groups make up the 64 currently configured window devices. To add the next group of windows, simply enter the command:

ltahoe# **MAKEDEV win2**

Note: This must be run as superuser, and you must be in the /*dev* directory. This will create the next set of 32 window devices. Now you have 96 windows. To make the next set of 32, enter the command:

ltahoe# **MAKEDEV win3**

This will make the last set of 32 devices giving you a total of 128 window devices.

This is currently the maximum number of window devices you may create.

8-19 Manipulating Text in a Window
Using Copy Then Paste

There will be many instances where you will want to move some text between windows or take a piece of the last command and re-use it. In your windows there are several ways to do this.

First, you will use the "cut and paste" facility that each window has. Let's say you want to copy a block of text between two windows. One window has some text displayed, the other is in the vi editor. To copy a block of text, you will need to place the block of text into a buffer. This is done by using the left mouse button to "mark" the beginning of the text block, and the middle mouse button to "mark" the end of the text block. When you click the middle button, the entire block of data will be highlighted. Then you can move the mouse button into the other window and use the window menu to select the "copy then paste" selection.

Here is an example of text transfer between windows. The window on the left contains data from a file called rhymes. You will move the Woodchuck rhyme from the left window to the right window which is in the vi editor and is in the insert mode.

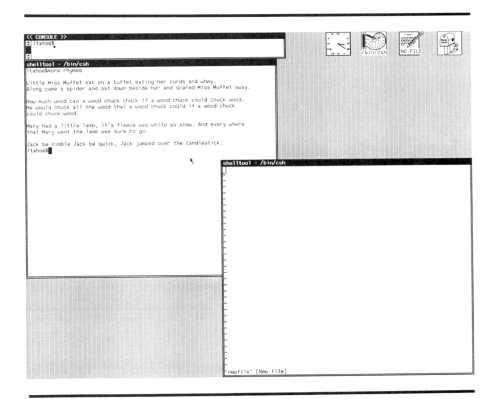

FIGURE 8.16. *Manipulating text between two SunView windows.*

First you will highlight the block of text you wish to move. You will click the left mouse button on the H in the beginning of the sentence. Now click middle on the period at the end of the sentence. The block of data will now be highlighted.

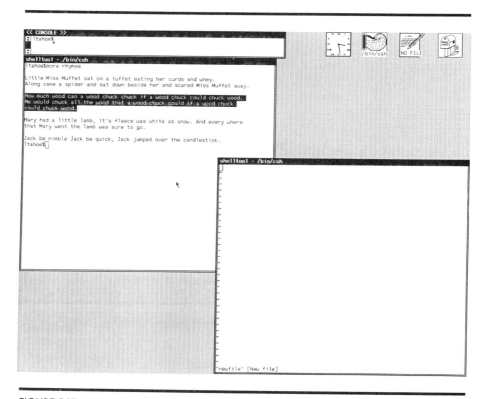

FIGURE 8.17. *Selecting text to be moved.*

Now you need to bring up the window sub-menu. To do this, click and hold the right mouse button inside the window you wish to move the text to. In this case, click and hold in the right window. You will now see the window sub-menu. While still holding the right mouse button down, move the pointer into the "copy then paste" selection and release the mouse button. (See Figure 8.18.)

Now the text is inserted into the right window. You could also use the "stuff" menu selection as well. (See Figure 8.19.)

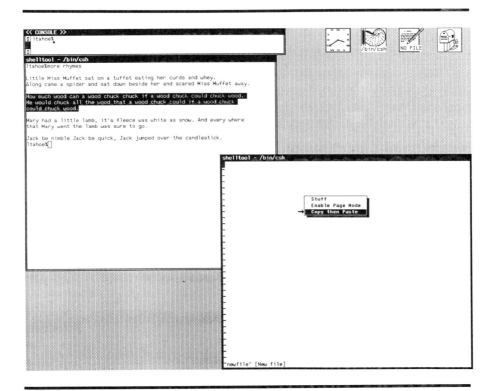

FIGURE 8.18.   *Copying text to a new window.*

Copy-Paste with the Keyboard

You can accomplish the same cut and paste functions with the keyboard that you can do with the menu selections. On the left hand side of the keyboard, you will see the L6 key and the L8 key. The L6 key is the equivalent of the copy key. The L8 key is the equivalent of the paste key. Try the same example as above but use the keyboard instead of the mouse.

Manipulating Text with the Mouse (multiple clicking)

You can edit the command line with the mouse in a variety of ways. The mouse has a special feature which allows you to select either a letter, a word, or the entire line by the number of times you

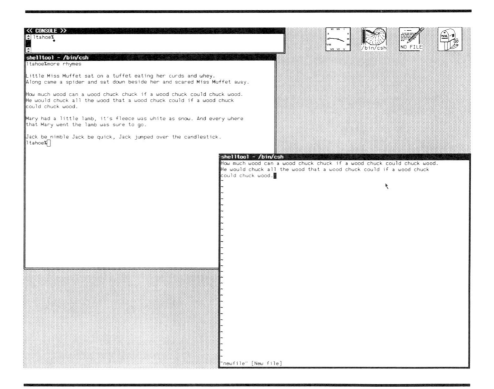

FIGURE 8.19. *Copied text placed into a new window.*

click the mouse button. If you have a line which contains a long string of words, you can select a letter by clicking the left mouse button once. If you wanted the entire word, you would click the left mouse button twice. You need to click quickly as the second button click only works if you click immediately after the first click. To select the entire line, click the left mouse button three times in a row. Remember to click quickly.

Once you have selected either the letter, word, or line, you can then stuff, copy then paste the selection to the current window or another window. The selection option works nicely when you make a mistake in a long command sequence and you need to take just a piece of the last command and make it a part of the current command. Try to make several text selections and place them into different windows. You will find this feature useful.

MailTool

9

9-1 Overview of MailTool

The sending and receiving of electronic mail or "e-mail" is one of the most widely used communications methods in the computer industry. With e-mail, you can send messages to every system user in your company as well as anywhere in the world. Before you get into world-wide e-mail, you must first learn how to send an e-mail message locally.

There are two ways to work with e-mail. One is with the program **mail,** the other is MailTool. Mail is executed from the command line and works with a tty interface, while MailTool has a SunView window interface. Since MailTool is much easier for the beginner to use, this chapter will focus on it.

When running in SunView, you have an application called MailTool. The MailTool icon is the one in the upper right hand corner of the SunView screen with the mailbox and flower.

Click the left mouse button on the MailTool icon. The Mail-Tool window is shown in Figure 9.1.

The MailTool window is divided into three sub-windows, with the frame header supplying related information. The three sub-windows are:

1. The Header List Window
2. The Command Panel Window
3. The Message Window.

9-2 The Frame Header

The frame header is the border at the top of the mailtool window. Here you will see messages like; No mail, New Mail, retrieving new mail, number of mail messages deleted, and the number of new messages.

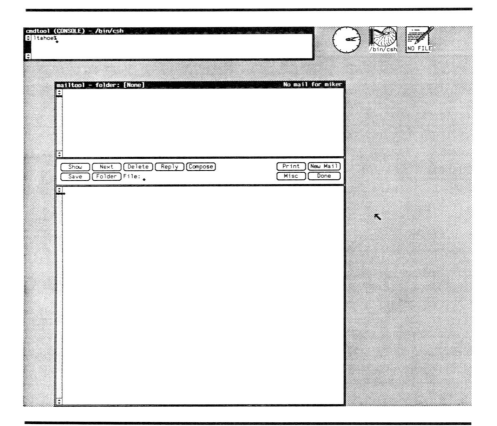

FIGURE 9-1. *Typical mailtool frame.*

9-3 Header List Window

The top section is called the Header List Window. Here is where you will see the header information about new mail messages. Look at the header message window in the following picture. (See Figure 9.2.)

In the example there are three mail messages. Two are from miker and one is from joe. Each line contains the following information, in order from left to right.

status

This can either be an N, U, >, or nothing. The N means that this message is a new message and has not been read yet.
The U stands for an unread message. This appears when you open your

```
mailtool - /usr/spool/mail/miker                          3 messages 2 new
        1 miker          Sun Dec  3 17:03   13/257    test
     >  2 miker          Sun Dec  3 17:12   13/287    mail example
     N  3 joe            Sun Dec  3 17:14   13/268    hi there
```

FIGURE 9-2. *The mailtool header list window.*

MailTool and read a few of the new messages you have received, and then close the MailTool application.

The > indicates the current message being viewed. A blank space means that you have read the mail and have not done anything with it such as save or delete.

message number

This is the order of the mail messages in your mail folder.

sender

This is the user who sent you the e-mail.

date

This is the date the mail was sent.

time

This is the time the message was sent.

message length

This field tells you the number of lines and the number of characters in the message.

subject

This is the subject the sender put in the subject field when he sent the message.

9-4 Command Panel Window

The middle section is the command panel window. This is where you will select functions in MailTool.

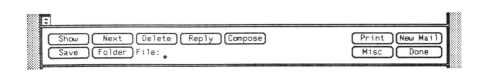

FIGURE 9-3. *The mailtool command panel window.*

Command Panel Buttons

Now you will see what each of the command panel buttons do.

Almost all of the buttons have menus associated with them. To look at what each buttons menu looks like, click right on each button and you will see the menu selections for each button.

Now you will learn each menu selection. As with all menus, if you click left on the button without bringing up the sub-menu, the option chosen will be the first option on the sub-menu list.

Note: Several of the menu items are self-explanatory and will not be covered here.

Show Figure 9-4 shows two choices. The first is "Show". This will display the mail message that is currently being pointed to in the header list window. You can point to a different message by clicking left on any of the other message lines and then clicking on show.

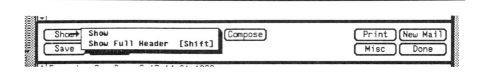

FIGURE 9-4. *View of the show sub-menu.*

The next option is "Show Full Header". This will display the entire message header for that mail message. Normally the bulk of a message header is eliminated because there is a lot of information that is not needed.

Save The save menu has two choices, these are Save and Copy. Clicking left on the Save button will save the message to a filename you select in the "File:" field in the command panel window. Once the message is saved, it will be deleted from the header list window.

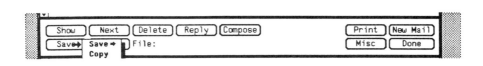

FIGURE 9-5. *View of the save sub-menu.*

The Save option also has a sub-menu which has some options to
view the next or previous message. You will on some menus see a
keyboard representation of that particular menu function. This is
only to show you what the keyboard equivalent would be. You do
not have to enter any keyboard commands when you select menu
items.

Next The next button will move you to the next letter in the
header list. If the current letter is the last one, "next" will go to the
previous letter. You can select the previous message by holding
down the right mouse button on the "next" selection. You will then
see a selection for "previous". This will display the previous mail
message.

Delete This will delete a mail message from the MailTool. When
you delete a mail message, you are actually just marking it for
removal. It will remain in the systems mail box or folder until
changes are committed. This is done when you finish a MailTool
session or commit the changes with the "done" button.

   If you accidentally delete a mail message you wanted to keep,
you can "undelete" the message by using the right mouse button
when selecting the delete item. You will then see an "undelete"
selection. This will only work if you have not committed the
changes prior to selection undelete.

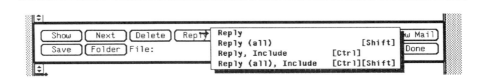

FIGURE 9-6. *View of the reply sub-menu.*

Reply You will use this button when you wish to reply to someone who has sent you a letter. When you select "reply", a composition window will automatically appear with the original sender's name already entered. There are three other ways to use reply. They are:

Reply (all) This will include all of the other people who received the mail message that you are replying to.

Reply (include) This will include a copy of the original mail with your reply.

Reply (all), include This will combine both of the above selections together to include the original mail and send it to all of the recipients.

Print Print will send a copy of the mail message to your regular printer. The entry for setting up the regular printer for mail is in the .mailrc file in your home directory.

New Mail The New Mail button will look for new mail that has arrived since you opened the MailTool session. If no new mail has arrived you will see a message appear in the border which states "No new mail for (username)". If new mail had arrived, then you will see the new messages appear in the message header window.

If you use the right mouse button with the New Mail selection, you will see the "commit" options to New Mail. The first is the default which retrieves new mail without committing any of the changes you have done so far. That is, if you have deleted any messages, you can still undelete them even though you have retrieved new mail. The other selection is to commit any changes you have made before you retrieve new mail.

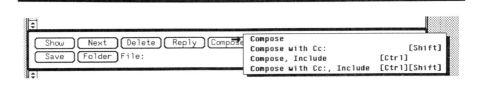

FIGURE 9-7. *View of the compose sub-menu.*

Compose Figure 9-7 shows the sub-menu where you can call up a composition window to generate a mail message. Compose has three other options, not unlike the reply selection has. The three selections are:

Compose with Cc: Here you will get a Cc: or carbon copy prompt which will allow you to send the mail to someone else, other than the user specified in the To: field.

You can specify MailTool to ask for Cc: everytime you bring up a composition window by setting the "askcc" variable in your .mailrc. See the section on the Defaults Editor for setting these functions.

Compose, Include Here you can compose a letter and include a selected mail message from the message header window.

Compose with Cc:, Include This will place a Cc: prompt in the composition window as well as include a selected message.

Folder The folder button will allow you to look at mail messages you have saved in your "folder" directory. You will learn more about folders in a little while since it requires more definition than can be given in these brief descriptions.

Misc The Misc button gives you three choices of commands to perform. Like the other buttons, the selections are displayed using the right mouse button. The selections are:

Change Directory This will change the directory which Mail-Tool looks for and saves letters in. Remember, the "File:" field only looks in the current directory unless you specify the path.

Source *.mailrc* When you make a change to the .mailrc file, the system will not recognize the changes until you "source" the file. Use this selection after making any changes.

Note: If you make a change to a variable that was previously set, i.e., was enabled and now is not, you will have to exit MailTool and start a new one. The system will learn new variables, but will not forget the old ones.

Preserve Normally in MailTool, a variable called "hold" is set so that mail messages you have already read are kept in the system mailbox until you delete or save them to a file. If you turn off this variable, you will have specified a file to keep all previously read messages. The preserve option will overide the "hold off" variable on a letter by letter basis so that you will retain the mail message in your system mailbox. As stated, if you have the hold variable "on", this option has no function.

Done The done button will close the MailTool back to iconic. There are three choices to the "done" selection. The first will commit the changes and close the MailTool to iconic. The second will commit the changes and quit the MailTool. The third will quit the MailTool without committing the changes.

9-5 The Message Window

The lower section is the message window. Here is where you will view the mail you receive.

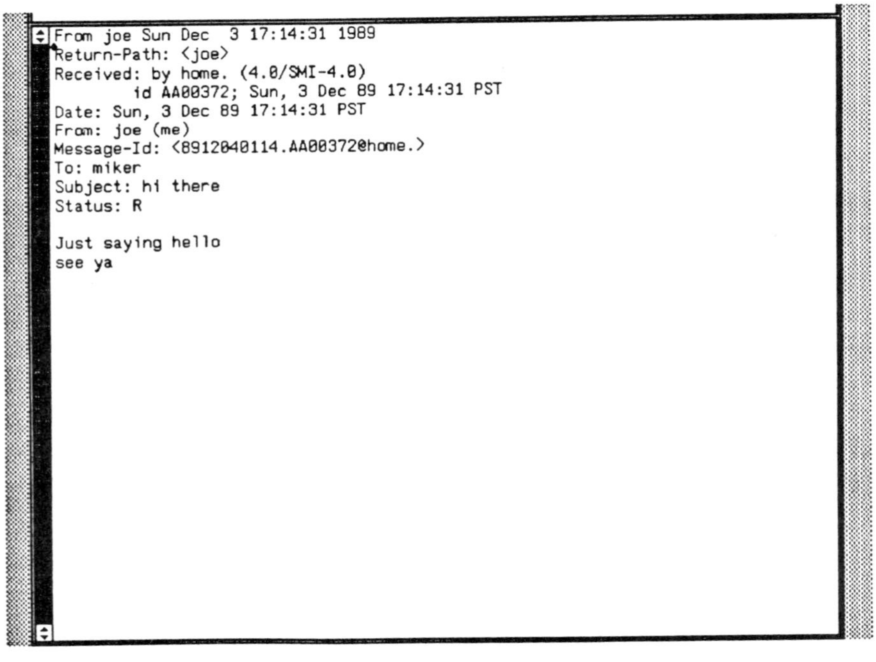

```
From joe Sun Dec  3 17:14:31 1989
Return-Path: <joe>
Received: by home. (4.0/SMI-4.0)
         id AA00372; Sun, 3 Dec 89 17:14:31 PST
Date: Sun, 3 Dec 89 17:14:31 PST
From: joe (me)
Message-Id: <8912040114.AA00372@home.>
To: miker
Subject: hi there
Status: R

Just saying hello
see ya
```

FIGURE 9-8. *View of the message window.*

9-6 Composing a Letter

When you send e-mail to a person or persons, you need to know a few things about them. The first is their username. This is the name they go by on their system. Usernames are unique in SunOS. For each user in your company who has access to a workstation will have a username, just as you now have a username. The second item you must know is the machinename. The third is, if the mail is to be sent to a remote site, the mail path to that site.

Same System

Begin by addressing mail to a user on the same system you are on.

If you are one of many clients of a server or workstation, you only need to address the mail to the username. For instance, if the person's username was pascale, you could address the mail to "pascale". When filling out the To: field, you would simply enter To:pascale

Local Network

If you are on separate systems on a local network, you will need to include the machinename as well as the username. When addressing includes the machinename, you must separate the two with the "@" symbol. The address would look like this if the username was pascale, and the machine name was crossfire.

To:pascale@crossfire

An easy way to remember this is that the "@" symbol is pronounced "at", so you could say "pascale at crossfire".

If your company is running the yellow pages database, you may only need the username, since the mail aliases database contains a list of which users are on what machines.

You should have a grasp of the concept now. Try to send a mail message to yourself just for practice.

To do this, select the compose button in the command panel window with the left mouse button. A composition window will now appear.

FIGURE 9-9. *View of selecting the compose button.*

Notice the message window is now split with the composition window on the bottom. Here you can reply to a mail message you received or send one of your own.

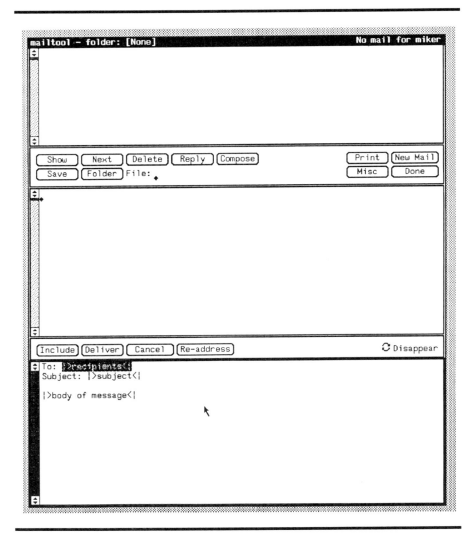

FIGURE 9-10. *View of the new composition window.*

Move the pointer into the composition window. The To: line will have a highlighted |<recipient>| after it. Now enter your username. It should appear on the To: line, and the |<recipient>| part will disappear. Now hold the control key down and then press the tab key. This will move you into the next field which is subject. Enter a subject title like "mail to myself". Control tab again and you will now be in the message area. You will see |<body of

message>|in this area. Now begin typing your message to yourself. Once you finish the message, move the pointer onto the "deliver" button and click the left button. The message is now on its way.

Viewing the Message

To see the message you sent to yourself, click the left mouse button on the new mail button. It may take a few moments for the new mail to arrive so be patient. If nothing appears, try the new mail button in a minute. You should now see your mail message listing in the header list window and your actual mail in the message window.

9-7 Folders

A wonderful feature of mailtool is the ability to save mail messages into a folder for better organization of your saved mail messages. For instance, if you are receiving mail from different people on three different subjects, say golf, tennis, and football, and you were to save every message to a different file, you may wind up with twenty or thirty files with different names.

A better way to save these messages is to save them by catagory, into a file which defines the messages. If you had a file named *tennis, golf,* and *football,* you could place each message for golf, into the golf file. Then you could call up all messages about golf by bringing up the golf folder. The messages will appear like normal mail and you can bring up any specific message you wish.

How is this done? Simple, in the Defaults Editor section, you define a variable called "folder" which would be the name of the directory which folder files are kept. You set this directory in the chapter on Editors. To enable the folder directory in the .mailrc file, you must source the .mailrc file. Do this by selecting the "source .mailrc" selection under "Misc" button in the command panel window. To place a mail message into your folder directory, simply enter at the file: line in the command panel window, the name of the file you wish to save the message to with a "+" sign before the filename, and click left on the save button. The "+" sign tells the system to place the message into the folder directory. It simplifies typing in a pathname in the file: field.

If you received a message about golf, you would enter

"+golf" after file: and click left on the save button. The golf message has now been saved into a file called "golf". Any other messages you receive about golf you can save to this file as well, since all messages are appended to the existing file.

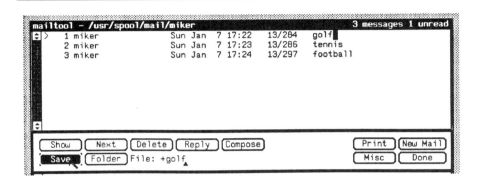

FIGURE 9-11. *Selecting the save button to save a message to a folder.*

If you wish to review the message about golf, you only need to hold down the right mouse button over the Folder button and select the folder name you wish to look at. For each file you have in the folder directory, a menu selection will appear.

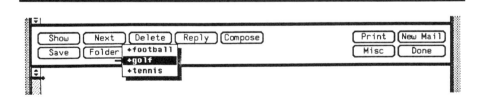

FIGURE 9-12. *Selecting a folder item for viewing.*

Release the right mouse button over the menu selection of the filename you wish to see. The file name will appear in the file: field in the command panel window. Click left on the Folder button to bring up the specified folder file. All messages which were saved to the golf folder will appear in the message header window.

Simply select which message you wish to look at with the left mouse button and click left on the Show button to display the message.

9-8 Remote Mail

There are ways to send e-mail to sites anywhere in the world (if they subscribe to outside communications with other companies). The two main networks are the ARPANET, and the UUCP network.

When sending mail to someone on the ARPANET, you would add the ARPANET name. For instance, Sun would be:

username@machinename.Sun.COM

The list of ARPANET names are:

- COM   This suffix is for commercial companies.
- EDU   This is for universities, the mail address would be:
            username@machinename.college.EDU
- ORG   This is for non profit organizations.
- GOV   This is for government agencies.
- MIL   This is for military agencies.

UUCP Mail

When sending mail on the UUCP network, you need to know the mail path to the other system. The UUCP network allows users to send mail via modems to remote sites. When sending mail to users on the UUCP network, you must know the mail path to the remote machine. The mail path to other machines can be thought of as post offices that your mail will have to travel through to get to its destination. Each post office has a name and the path to each post office is separated by a "!" called a ("bang"). If you wanted to send a mail message to someone at a system called waterfall, you would need to know the names of the intermediate machines (post offices) that the mail would pass through. Say the intermediate machines are "pool", "stream", and "fountain", and the username at waterfall was pascale. The mail path to pascale would be:

pool!stream!fountain!waterfall!pascale

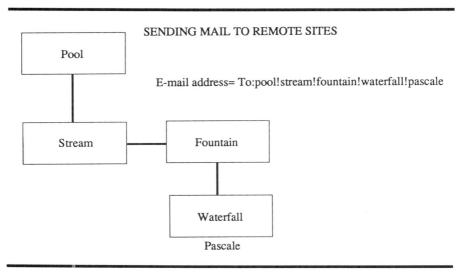

FIGURE 9-13. *Path to a remote mail site called waterfall.*

To find the paths to remote sites that you are unsure of, ask your systems administrator.

9-9 Mail Aliases

You have the ability in mail to create "aliases" which contain the names of other users to which you may send mail frequently. An alias is a list of users tied together with a common name. If you had a ski club which had several users in it, you could create an alias called "ski" which which would contain all of the users' names. Then, when you want to send mail to the ski club, you would address the mail to the alias, in this case "ski".

Try creating an alias for practice. There are two ways to create an alias, one is in your *.mailrc* file, the other is in */etc/aliases*. The */etc/aliases* file is easier to use and allows other users to use it as well.

An entry in the */etc/aliases* file would look like this:

ski: miker@ltahoe, pascale@telephone, woody@squirrel

You can edit this file with vi or any other editor you like. (You must be the superuser in order to edit this file.)

When you edit the file, it will already contain some example aliases. Go to the bottom of the file and create your own. All entries should be separated with a ",", but do not put a comma after the last entry, or the system will think there is still another entry and the alias will fail.

Once you have edited the file, you will need to run a command called "**newaliases**". This will inform the system of the new alias.

`ltahoe% newaliases`

If the alias resided on a machine called ltahoe, and someone on a remote machine wanted to use the ski alias, they would only have to address the mail to "ski@ltahoe" This would then send a copy of the mail to all users listed in the ski alias on ltahoe.

Mailrc Aliases You can set up aliases in your *.mailrc* file located in your home directory. To do this edit your .mailrc file and create an alias that is similar to the type of alias you created in your .cshrc file. Here is an example entry that would send mail to three users named in an alias called golfers:

alias golfers pascale@crossfire dave@parl joe@teeoff

When sending mail to this alias, you would simply address the mail To:golfers

If you make changes to your .mailrc file, you must source the file so the system knows about the changes. Do this by selecting the "source .mailrc" option under the "Misc" button in the command panel window.

The system will check your *.mailrc* file for the alias golfers and send mail to the users listed in the alias. Be sure to separate the usernames with spaces and not commas. Only you can use the aliases in your *.mailrc* file. Use the */etc/aliases* file if you wish others to use the alias.

There are many other uses for aliases. See the man page on aliases for a complete listing of options.

Networking

10

10-1 Using the Network

Of all the advantages that your Sun system has to offer, networking is one of the greatest.

Using the network to your advantage is not as difficult as you may think. There are many simple commands and applications that even a novice user can learn in a few short minutes. Take a look at what a networked system really is and what it can do for you.

What Is a Network?

A network is a means for computers and other devices to communicate with each other. Machines connected by a network can share files and printers, execute commands remotely, share disk space, and transfer information at the touch of a button. Most Sun users are on a network of some kind, either linked to other Sun systems, or to various other types of computers.

A simple network (or local area network) can be a group of machines all connected together. You may also be connected to many other networks that are linked together. These are referred to as "wide area networks". Wide area networks can not only span a local building or set of buildings, but also can spread out over the entire country or world. Such networks, like the ARPANET (Advanced Research Projects Agency Network), are used by users across the country to exchange information and programs.

Take a look at a simple local area network. (See Figure 10.1.)

10-2 NFS

Machines must know how to communicate with each other before they can actually interact. This interaction is referred to as a protocol. NFS (Network File System) was developed by Sun, to allow systems to access and share files across a network. This way, you have the ability to share files or programs which reside on another

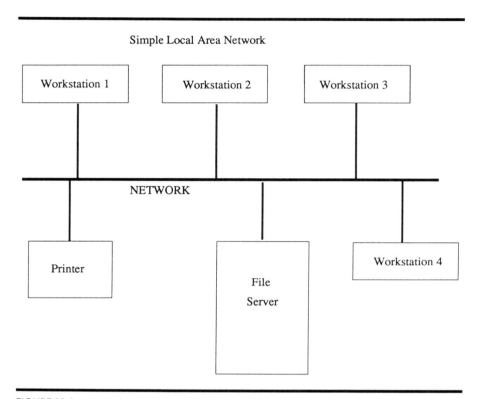

Simple Local Area Network

FIGURE 10-1. *View of a simple local area network.*

machine, yet they appear to be as if they are on your machine. File systems can be "NFS mounted" onto your system from file servers or other workstations. This way you can have one system contain software and applications, then have all of the other systems utilize them as if they were actually on their own system. This will be explained in detail a little later.

10-3 Yellow Pages (YP)

Note: Yellow Pages (YP), is now referred to as NIS or Network Information Services.

As your network grows, it becomes increasingly difficult to control all of the machine names, user names, passwords, and other network control files. It was because of this reason that Sun developed a distributed database lookup system called yp. It provides a means by which all systems can look up information about other systems and users, without needing to have the information on each system itself. For instance, if you have several networks with about 20 to 30 systems each, and all of the systems needed to communicate with each other, you would need to update each and every system, anytime a new system was added. With say four networks, that is 120 systems to make changes to. Your system administrator will have many gray hairs.

The yp system provides all systems on the networks with the information needed to establish links with each other.

Each system on a network has a network address, just like your house has an address. The yp database contains a file that holds all of the addresses for each system on the network. A small list of yp files might be: hosts, password, netgroup, and aliases.

Ypbind-Ypserv

The yp service is run by two daemons called "ypserv" and "ypbind". A server which contains a copy of the database would run the ypserv daemon. All systems which need to access the database would run the ypbind daemon. The ypbind daemon connects your system to a server which is running ypserv. When you need to get information from the yp database, ypbind maintains contact with the ypserver and retrieves the information.

You can check to see if the daemon is running on your system by using the "**ps**" command, and the **grep** command.

If ypbind was running, the system would respond with:

```
ltahoe% ps -ax |grep ypbind
213 ? S 0:00 ypbind
```

Note: Not all companies run the yp service. Talk to your systems administrator to find out if you do.

10-4 YP Commands

There are a few commands the user can use to look up information in the yp database. Here are some you will find useful:

ypmatch This command allows you to look up an entry in a specified yp file. The syntax of the ypmatch command is:

ypmatch key mapname

So to check the host number of the system named ltahoe:

```
ltahoe% ypmatch ltahoe hosts
129.144.89.54 ltahoe
```

ypwhich This command will tell you which ypserver your system is bound to. To use the ypwhich command, simply enter:

```
ltahoe% ypwhich
genesis
```

Here the machine "genesis" is the ypserver to the system ltahoe.

If your system was not running ypbind, you would see an error message like this:

```
ltahoe% ypwhich
ypwhich: ltahoe is not running ypbind
```

yppasswd Here you can change your yp password entry. Normally it is the same as your local machines entry. In this way you can log into other machines and still use your regular system password. To change your yp password entry, enter the command:

```
ltahoe% yppasswd
Changing yppasswd for miker
Old yp password:
New password:
Retype new password:
yellow pages passwd changed
```

The yp database is now updated with your new password.

ypcat Here you can ask for a specific map in the yp database to be displayed. To use ypcat, enter the command ypcat, followed by the map name you wish to see. If you only want to see a specific entry and not the entire map, pipe the output to grep and ask for a specific entry.

```
ltahoe% ypcat passwd | grep miker
miker:kdps/72hg?:4801:30:Mike
Russo:/home/miker:/bin/csh
```

In this instance the yp password entry for myself has been displayed out of the database.

If you had only specified passwd after **ypcat,** you would have seen the entire yp password file.

10-5 Mounting Remote File Systems

Earlier you learned about NFS and how it allows you to mount file systems onto your system. Let's take a look at how this is done.

Say you have a department which utilizes a spreadsheet software that all of the users will need. It would save a lot of disk space if your department only had to maintain one copy of the software, rather than have a copy for each system in the department. To do this you will "mount" the software onto your system.

```
shelltool - /bin/csh
ltahoe% more /etc/fstab
/dev/sd0a / 4.2 rw,nosuid 1 1
/dev/sd0g /usr 4.2 rw 1 2
/dev/sd0h /home 4.2 rw 1 3
ltahoe%
```

FIGURE 10-2. *Common* /etc/fstab *file.*

In the directory called */etc*, there is a file called *"fstab"* (File System Table). This file tells the system where to get the remote file systems from. The basic file will contain your system's hard disk information, or client information if your system is diskless.

Here is a basic */etc/fstab* file for a diskfull system.

To add a remote file system mount on your system, you will need to edit the fstab file with the correct information. (You must be root in order to edit this file.) The information required is:

machinename:	filesystem mountpoint type option freq pass
machinename	The machine name that the file system resides on.
filesystem	Remote file system. (Like */home/games*)
mountpoint	Directory on your system where the mount will reside.
type	Type of mount. Usually "4.2" for disk devices, "nfs" for remote file systems.
option	Any options to the mount. There are many options to mounts. The basic ones are either "hard" or "soft". With the hard

mounted file system, should the remote system go down, your
system will not allow any activity until the remote system is
accessible again. A soft mount will background the mounted
file system and issue an error stating that the mount has failed
and is retrying. It is recommended that soft mounts be used.
Another option is whether the remote file system will be
mounted read only or read-write. If it is read only, you will
need to insert "ro", if you are mounting read-write, you will
enter "rw".

freq   This is the interval in days between dumps. This is always 0
on nfs mounted file systems.

pass   Fsck pass number. This is the order that fsck will perform
disk checks. On nfs mounted file systems, it is always 0.
NOTE! If you have a system with multiple disk controllers,
you can have the system run fsck in tandem with another
controller on parallel partitions. This saves time when the
system is running fsck. Ask your systems adminstrator to see
if you can do this.

Make an fstab entry to mount a directory which contains
spreadsheet software from a system called spring. The software
resides on the remote system in a directory named */home/
spreadsheet.* You will mount it onto your system on a directory
under */home* called *utilities.* (You can name the mount point anything you wish.)

You need to edit the *fstab* file in */etc.* (You must be root in
order to edit this file.)

```
shelltool - /bin/csh
/dev/sd0a / 4.2 rw,nosuid 1 1
/dev/sd0g /usr 4.2 rw 1 2
/dev/sd0h /home 4.2 rw 1 3
#
spring:/home/spreadsheet  /home/utilities nfs ro,soft 0 0
~
~
~
~
~
~
~
"/etc/fstab" 3 lines, 83 characters
```

FIGURE 10-3. *Adding a new entry to the /etc/fstab file.*

In this example, you have mounted from the machine "spring", the file system */home/spreadsheet,* onto the local file system */home/utilities.* The mount is the type "nfs" and is a soft mount. It is mounted read only since you will not need to write to the remote file system, and will not have any fsck checking done.

Now that you have edited the fstab file, you must create the directory on your system that the remote file system will be mounted to. In this example you must create the directory "utilities" under */home.*

```
ltahoe% mkdir /home/utilities
```

If you do not create the mount point directory, and attempt to mount the file system, the system will respond with an error message that states:

```
mount:spring:/home/spreadsheet on /home/utilities:
no such file or directory
mount:giving up on /home/utilities
```

Mount Command

You have now edited the fstab file and created your mount point. Now you must run the "**mount**" command. The **mount** command will look at the fstab and mount the new file system. Mount can be used to generate temporary mounts, or long term mounts with the fstab file. To activate your mount from the fstab entry, simply enter the command **mount -a** (for all). You must be root to execute the mount command.

```
ltahoe# mount -a
```

This will mount all entries in the fstab file. If the current entries are already mounted, it will go on to the next entry in the file.

If you look at the directory */home/utilities,* you will find all of the files and software that resides on the remote system spring, under */home/spreadsheet.* You can now utilize the software and even copy the files to a directory on your system.

Temporary Mounts

You can generate temporary mounts with the mount command without editing the fstab file. To do this, you must first create the mount point directory. Then, if you wanted your spring example to be a temporary one, you would enter the command:

```
ltahoe# mount spring:/home/spreadsheet /home/utilities nfs ro,soft 0 0
```

(Remember you must be root to mount file systems.)

This mount will stay in effect until you either reboot your system, or use the "umount" command.

You can check to see which file systems you are currently mounting by using the mount command without options. Simply enter the command:

```
ltahoe% mount
/dev/sd0a on / type 4.2 (rw,nosuid)
/dev/sd0g on /usr type 4.2 (rw)
/dev/sd0h on /home type 4.2 (rw)
```

You do not have to be root to use the mount command without any options. The mount command is located under */etc*. You may not have this path identified for yourself and will get an error message that will say "command not found". Just specify the path to the mount command and it will work fine.

Umount Command

The umount command will unmount currently mounted file systems. In the spring example, you mounted a remote file system to */home/utilities*. If you wanted to unmount that file system, you would enter the command:

```
ltahoe# umount /home/utilities
```

The system would then unmount */home/utilities*. (You must be root to use umount as well.)

You can unmount a specific file system with the -h option to the umount command. The -h stands for "hosts" and will dismount any nfs mount from the hostname specified. If you wanted to unmount just spring, you would enter the command:

```
ltahoe# umount -h spring
```

The system would unmount only the spring entry from the currently mounted file systems.

10-6 The Automounter

Sun has developed a utility which will mount remote file systems for you without having to become root, or having to enter mount command options. The mounting of the remote file system is invisible to you and the system will unmount the file system after a certain period of inactivity.

The automounter may be a little tricky to use and you should consult your systems administrator for assistance, since each company may have different yp systems and network capabilities.

If you think you are running the standard yp service and you wish to use the automounter, you would need to start the automount service on your system. To do this, an example would be:

ltahoe# **automount -m /net -hosts /homes -passwd**

The /net -hosts will mount named machines listed in the hosts database file from the yp database. The /homes -passwd will mount users' home directories from the password database file. (You must be root to start the automounter. You can place this at the end of your */etc/rc.local* file to start the automounter each time you reboot your system.)

Now if you wanted to look at the file system /var/spool on a remote machine called largo, you would simply enter the command:

ltahoe% **ls /net/largo/var/spool**

Notice you use */net* in the path. This tells the automounter to mount the named file system with the machine name after */net*.

The output of your ls command would give you a listing of the contents of the */var/spool* directory on a machine called largo.

You can also look at a user's home directory by specifying */homes* in the path followed by the username of the person whom you wish to mount.

Let's say you want to look at a file in the home directory of a user called pascale. You would enter the command:

ltahoe% **ls /homes/pascale**

The system would then list the contents of pascale's home directory.

You could use any of the standard commands like **cd, ls, more,** etc. with the automounter. For instance,

```
ltahoe% more /homes/pascale/admin.contact
system adminstrator-----lance x12345
```

Look at the man page on automount for an indepth description of options and usage. As stated before, you should consult your systems administrator for assistance in setting up the automount function.

Note!!! In order for your system to mount another systems files, the other system must be "exporting" that particular file system. This means that the remote system is allowing other users to have access to its files. Talk to your system administrator to find out what other machines are exporting. If you try to automount a file system that is not exported, you would see an error message like:

```
ltahoe% ls /homes/pascale
homespascale: No such file or directory
```

This may seem like an obscure error message, but it is the message that appears in instances of non-exportation.

10-7 Using RCP

Earlier you were shown how to mount other file systems to utilize and copy files from one system to another. But what if you only want to copy one file or a single directory? It would be too much trouble to have to mount the other system just to copy the file. Well don't worry, there is a command called "**rcp**" (remote copy) which will allow you to copy files from one system to the other.

Say you want to copy the file called "*jokes*" from a system called "jetski" to your system. You must specify the path that *jokes* resides in on the remote system, and the path to where you wish to put it on your system. If the file "*jokes*" resides on the system "jetski" under the path: */home/funny/jokes*, and you wish to put it on your system under a directory path: */home/goodstuff*. The syntax for this would be:

```
ltahoe% rcp jetski:/home/funny/jokes /home/goodstuff
```

If you list the contents of the directory goodstuff under */home*, you would find the new file called jokes.

You can also copy from your machine to another by reversing the command. If you wanted to copy your new jokes file to another system called genesis, you would simply enter the command:

```
ltahoe% rcp /home/goodstuff/jokes genesis:/directoryname
```

If you are in the directory which contains the file *jokes*, you do not need to specify the path to *jokes*.

```
ltahoe% rcp jokes genesis:/directoryname
```

You need to watch out for permission problems when copying to other users' systems. If you try to rcp a file into someone else's home directory, and you do not have write permission to that directory, the system will respond with a "permission denied" message. This message will also appear if you try to write to a directory like */etc* or other system-owned directories. The best way to ensure that the file will get there ok is to copy it to the other system's */tmp* directory. This way you or the other user can always move it to the correct directory once it is on the system.

Copying Directories with -r

When you want to copy an entire directory to another system, you will need to use the "-r" option. This option, which means "recursive", will copy all of the files and any subdirectories under the specified directory. The syntax for this is:

```
ltahoe% rcp -r jetski:/home/goodstuff /home/mystuff
```

If you looked onto the directory mystuff, you would see a new directory called *goodstuff* with all of the files under it.

Note! When you copy directories with **rcp**, you do not retain the original permissions or ownership. Refer to the man page on **rcp** to find out other options and capabilities.

10-8 Logging into Remote Systems with rsh

You can log into other systems from yours with the rsh (Remote Shell) command. The **rsh** command can do several things for you. You can remotely log into another system, or you can execute commands on another system.

To log into another system, simply enter the command:

```
ltahoe% rsh vino
password:
vino%
```

You are now logged onto vino as if you were at sitting at vino's terminal. Here you can execute commands, or even log into other systems from vino. To leave the system vino, simply enter "**exit**"

```
vino% exit
ltahoe%
```

Note! When the ignoreeof variable is not set on the remote system, you can also exit by typing a **Ctrl D**.

Remote Commands with rsh

You can execute commands remotely with **rsh** by specifying the command you wish to run after the machine name. If you wanted to perform an ls of the directory /home/wine on a system called vino, you could execute the command:

```
ltahoe% rsh vino ls /home/wine
red white pink other
```

Try to execute other commands on remote systems to familiarize yourself with **rsh.**

10-9 Useful Network Commands

There are several useful commands to find out information about other users and systems on the network. Here are some commands you may want to try out.

finger	Find out the time a user was working on his system.
ping	See if a remote system is up.
rup	Check uptime and load average on a particular system or systems on the net.
rusers	List users on a remote system.
showmount	Show machines which are mounting file systems on a specified system.

Here is how each command is used.

Finger

This is a very useful command for finding out if a user you want to reach is still at their system, or has been absent for a while. The command is called "**finger**" and it does just that! It will finger the person on his or her system and check for activity. The syntax for this command is:

```
lthaoe% finger username@machinename
```

Example:
```
ltahoe% finger miker@ltahoe
```

```
ltahoe
Login name: miker                       In real life: Michael Russo
Directory: /home/ltahoe/miker           Shell: /bin/csh
On since Aug 31 08:42:24 on console
New mail received Thu Aug 31 14:27:14 1989;
unread since Thu Aug 31 14:27:15 1989
No Plan.
Login name: miker                       In real life: Michael Russo
Directory: /home/ltahoe/miker           Shell: /bin/csh
On since Aug 31 14:03:10 on ttyp0       31 minutes Idle Time
Login name: miker                       In real life: Michael Russo
Directory: /home/ltahoe/miker           Shell: /bin/csh
On since Aug 31 14:03:21 on ttyp1       5 minutes 21 seconds Idle Time
Login name: miker                       In real life: Michael Russo
Directory: /home/ltahoe/miker           Shell: /bin/csh
On since Aug 31 14:03:27 on ttyp5       1 minute 16 seconds Idle Time
```

Note that it tells you the last time a keystroke was performed in a shell as well as when the last e-mail message was read. There are several options to finger which can be explored in the man page for the finger command.

Ping

The **ping** command will tell you if another system is alive or not. The syntax of the "**ping**" command is: **ping** (**systemname**) An example of the **ping** command is:

```
ltahoe% ping hoopster
hoopster is alive
```

If the machine you want to ping is down, or the network is not functioning, the response would be:

```
ltahoe% ping hoopster
no response from hoopster
```

The -s option to ping is useful if you want to see if the network is running slow. This will give you the round trip time to the other system and back.

ltahoe% **ping -s hoopster**

```
PING hoopster: 56 data bytes
64 bytes from 129.144.89.30: icmp_seq=0. time=0. ms
64 bytes from 129.144.89.30: icmp_seq=1. time=0. ms
64 bytes from 129.144.89.30: icmp_seq=2. time=0. ms
64 bytes from 129.144.89.30: icmp_seq=3. time=0. ms
64 bytes from 129.144.89.30: icmp_seq=4. time=0. ms
```

Rup

This command is used to see the uptime and load average on a remote system. To use the rup command, simply enter rup followed by the system name you wish to investigate.

ltahoe% **rup hoopster**
```
hoopster up 7 days, 14 hours, load average: 0.37,
0.24, 0.01
```

Rusers

The rusers command will display the users who are currently logged into a remote system. The usage of the command is:

ltahoe% **rusers hoopster**
```
pascale miker lancej
```

For a more detailed listing, you can use the -l option to rusers. This will tell you port name, login time, and idle time.

ltahoe% **rusers -l hoopster**
```
pascale hoopster:console  Jan 10 08:30 3:21
miker   hoopster:ttyd7    Jan 10 09:00 1:12
lancej  hoopster:ttyd5    Jan 10 09:24 8:49
```

Showmount

This command will show you who is mounting file systems on your system. Let's say you have this wonderful games directory on my system. If you wanted to see who was mounting this directory on my system, you would run the showmount command:

```
ltahoe% showmount -a
hoopster:/home/games
crossre:/home/games
arwen:/home/games
```

The -a option will show "all" systems mounting files on your machine.

There is an "-e" option which will show you what file systems you are exporting and to whom you are exporting them to. Exporting means that you are allowing certain machines access to file systems on your machine.

```
ltahoe% showmount -e
export list for ltahoe
/home/games everyone
/home/demo hoopster,arwen,zeplin
```

In this case ltahoe is exporting */home/games* to everyone, and */home/demo* only to the machines hoopster, arwen, and zeplin.

Backing Up Your System

If your workstation is diskless, you will not have to worry about backing up your files. The system administrator will have backups run on the client server regularly. If you are a diskfull workstation, that is, one with a local hard disk for main storage, chances are that you will need to backup your files regularly. If your company runs full backups on the diskfull systems you can skip this section. If not, then read on.

If you are responsible for your workstation, you should run backups each night, or at least as often as your files change. This is important because should you have a disk failure or corruption, or if you accidentally erase a file that you still need, you can recover the data. If you don't do daily backups, you wouldn't be the first person to lose hours or even months worth of work.

11-1 Using Dump

There are several ways to archive the data on your system with the **dump** command. You should always have at least a full level 0 dump for each month with incrementals on a daily and weekly basis.

The **dump** command works on a simple basis. A 0 level dump places all of the data for a specific file system onto a tape. It can be either a cartridge tape, or a half inch reel tape. All other dumps are called incremental dumps and only archive data which has changed since the last lower level dump.

The term "level" for dumps means that the system will only archive data which has only recently changed. Levels range from 0 through 9. A 0 level dump will archive all data on a file system. A level 1 will archive all data which has changed since the last level 0. If you run a level 3 after a level 2, the system will only archive data which has changes since the level 2. You can use many combinations of dump levels but they all basically mean the same thing: the system will archive any data which has changed since the last lower level dump.

To understand how the different levels of dump interact, it is important to know the purpose of the */etc/dumpdates* file. When the 'u' option to the **dump** command is used in the command line, as seen below, the */etc/dumpdates* file records the date of the most recent dump of each level. For example:

```
ltahoe% more /etc/dumpdates
/dev/rsd0a 9 Wed Feb 31 19:06:25 1990
/dev/rsd0g 9 Wed Feb 31 19:07:46 1990
/dev/rsd0h 9 Wed Feb 31 19:08:48 1990
/dev/rsd0a 5 Mon Mar 19 23:34:18 1990
/dev/rsd0g 5 Mon Mar 19 23:35:24 1990
/dev/rsd0h 5 Mon Mar 19 23:36:12 1990
/dev/rsd0a 0 Fri Mar 16 22:14:36 1990
/dev/rsd0g 0 Fri Mar 16 22:15:27 1990
/dev/rsd0h 0 Fri Mar 16 22:22:49 1990
```

Looking at levels more closely, you can see how they interact. The levels of dump are from 0 through 9. Depending on which level dump you run, all files are copied to the tape which has been modified since the last lower level dump. For instance, there are many options to the **dump** command, but you will only look at the ones you need to accomplish your dump.

A common practice is to generate a 0 level of the system files, since they rarely change once the system is installed. Then run dumps only on the filesystems that change, such as your home directory or your database directory.

Run a 0 level dump on your home file system. In this example you will be dumping to a 1/4 inch cartridge tape. To accomplish this, run the command:

```
ltahoe# dump 0cfu /dev/nrst0 /home
```

The c, f, and u options are for:

```
c = cartridge tape
f = device to dump to. In this case /dev/rst0
u = update the /etc/dumpdates file.
0 = represents the level of the dump (0 through 9).
```

It is important to note that when doing a full level 0 of your system, often more than one cartridge or reel tape is needed. Always read the manufacturer's specifications provided with all tape media. If it is obvious that not all of your workstations' file systems will fit onto one tape you have a couple of options. You may wish to dump each file system to individual tapes for easy data retrieval, or to conserve tape, you may run them consecutively. The dump command allows for this nicely by simply prompting you to load a second tape. For example:

```
ltahoe# dump 0cfu /dev/nrst0 /home
DUMP: Date of this level 0 dump: Wed Mar 21 13:14:
02 1990
DUMP: Date of last level 0 dump: the epoch
DUMP: Dumping /dev/rsd0h (/home) to /dev/nrst0
DUMP: mapping (Pass I) regular les
DUMP: mapping (Pass II) directories
DUMP: estimated 262872 blocks (128.36MB) on 3.00
tape(s).
DUMP: dumping (Pass III) directories
DUMP: dumping (Pass IV) regular les
DUMP: 19.46% done, nished in 0:20
DUMP: Tape rewinding
DUMP: Change Tapes: Mount tape # 2
DUMP: NEEDS ATTENTION: Is the new tape mounted and
 ready to go?:
(yes'' or no'')
```

Dump Schedule

Now the system will be archiving all data to tape. Once this is done, you will want to run incrementals each night. A common schedule for incrementals is:

	Sun	Mon	Tue	Wed	Thu	Fri
Week 1:	0	5	5	5	5	3
Week 2:		5	5	5	5	3
Week 3:		5	5	5	5	3
Week 4:		5	5	5	5	3

With this schedule, you would only have to restore at most three tapes, if a disk failed or you lost your home directory.

11-2 Using Restore

Let's say you accidentally removed an important directory which contained the information on a project your boss wants tomorrow. It is Wednesday in week 1 of the month. If you have been doing your backups, you would not even have to skip a heartbeat.

All you need to do is take the 0 level and last incremental tape from Tuesday and begin the restore process.

In the event that you have dumped more than one file system onto a single tape, you must first position the tape to the correct file system before beginning the restore.

Lets say that when you did your last level 0 you were able to dump /, /usr, and /home (in that order) on a single tape. Dump places an end of file mark at the end of each file system dumped to tape. Therefore, each file system represents one FILE on the tape. The first file on the tape always represents file 0, the second is file 1, the third is file 2, etc.

In this example, you would first of all need to position the tape to /home, the third file on the tape. This is done with the 'mt' command as shown:

ltahoe% **mt -f /dev/nrst0 fsf 2**

To recover a directory from tape, follow these steps:

1) Become superuser

2) cd to a place where there is enough room to do the restore. Usually your home directory.

3) mkdir *restore* and cd to *restore.*

4) position the tape with the '**mt**' command if necessary.

5) execute the following command:

ltahoe# **restore ivf /dev/rst0**

The options to this are:

i = interactive (specify the directory to be restored)
v = verbose (show each file as it is restored)
f = device to restore from

The system will display the following:

```
ltahoe% restore ivf /dev/rst0
Verify tape and initialize maps
Tape block size is 126
Dump date: Sun Jan 7 16:08:18 1990
Dumped from: Wed Dec 31 16:00:00 1969
Extract directories from tape
Initialize symbol table. restore >
```

At this point you need to specify which directory you wish to add to the extract list. If the directory is a few levels down, you can **cd** into the directory and ls the next directory until you get to the one you want. Then simply type:

```
restore>add (directoryname)
```

After this command, you can **ls** again and you will see an "*" next to the directory you added. You can continue to add other directories if you wish, or just extract the one specified.

To extract the directory from the tape, simply enter "**extract**" after the `restore >` prompt.

```
restore > extract
```

The system will display the following:

```
restore > extract
Extract requested files
You have not read any tapes yet.
Unless you know which volume your file(s) are on you
should start with the last volume and work towards the
first.
Specify next volume #:
```

Enter 1 for volume number if the file system to be restored from is on one tape. If the file system you need to restore from is on more than one tape (you were prompted for tape#2 when making the dump tape), load the last tape first, i.e. tape#2. You will be prompted for tape#1 when the data is done being extracted from the second tape.

At the completion of every level of restore the last thing you need to do before quitting out of restore is set the ownership of the files. For example:

```
Set directory mode, owner, and times.
set owner/mode for .'? yn  n
restore >q
ltahoe#
```

If you were to type 'y' before quitting restore, the files that you restored would be owned by root. By typing 'n' you set the ownership to the state they were in at the time of the dump.

Once the directory is extracted from the tape, you will need to get any changes made to the directory from the incremental. Use the same procedure when restoring the incremental that you did for the level 0.

After the directory is restored from the 0 level and incremental, you will need to copy it to the appropriate directory from /restore. You can either move, or copy it to its rightful home.

Note: The example given was to restore an entire directory up to the date it was removed. If you only need to restore one or several FILES, considerable time can be saved if you know the date of the last modifications to the desired files. Due to the fact that the date of the file is changed each time a file is edited or created, working or new files will be dumped on that night's incremental. Therefore, if you accidentally removed a file and not a directory, you could retrieve the entire file from the previous night's backup and not have to go all the way back to the level 0.

There are many variations in doing restores. You should read the man page on restore to understand the many options available to you.

11-3 Using Tar

There are times when you will wish to place some files or directories onto a tape. This is easily accomplished with the "**tar**" (tape archive) command. The **tar** command will take specified files and place them on the tape device you specify. There are numerous options to the tar command which can get a little confusing. Here we will go over the basic tar command for placing files onto a tape and restoring them back onto your disk.

The basic options to the tar command are:

c   create tar file
v   verbose output (show what is going on)
f   tape device if not standard output
x   extract tar file
t   show table of contents

Now try to copy a file called testfile to the tape device called rst0 (standard 1/4″ tape drive).

```
ltahoe% cd /home
ltahoe% tar cvf /dev/rst0 testfile
tar cvf /dev/rst0 testfile
a testfile 1 blocks
ltahoe%
```

If you wish to see the contents of the tape, you can use the "t" option to tar.

```
ltahoe% tar tf /dev/rst0
testfile
ltahoe%
```

To extract the tarfile into your */tmp* directory, you will use the "x" option.

```
ltahoe% cd /tmp
ltahoe% tar xvf /dev/rst0
x testfile, 450 bytes, 1 tape blocks
ltahoe% ls
testfile
ltahoe%
```

You can archive entire directories or just a simple file with tar. To archive your entire home directory to a tar tape, simply cd to your parent directory and enter the following command:

```
ltahoe% tar cvf /dev/rst0 .
```

The "." (dot), represents the current working directory.

Now the entire contents of your home directory will be on the tape.

Note: Be sure you have enough space on the tape! A standard cartridge tape will hold about 40 megabytes of data. If your home directory exceeds this amount the tar will fail.

Printing a File

12

12-1 Using LPR

The printing of a file, that is producing a piece of paper with the contents of the file printed on it, is quite simple in itself. To system administrators it can sometimes be complicated and frustrating. For the user, it is as simple as executing the **lpr** (line printer) command.

The **lpr** command is your general print command when attempting to produce a hard copy of a file or document. A hard copy is produced when you output a file to a printing device such as a laserwriter or line printer.

The **lpr** command is simple to use as you can see in the following example:

```
ltahoe% lpr "filename"
```

Say you have a file called *phonelist* on my system and you want to produce a hard copy of it so you can take it home with you. The command would be:

```
ltahoe% lpr phonelist
```

The printer would then print out the file called *phonelist*.

There are several conditions that must be established on your system before the **lpr** command will work. Your system administrator should have set up the printing environment for you. You will see a little of what the administrator will have done but not in great detail as this is beyond the scope of this book.

There is a file in the */etc* directory called *printcap*. This file tells the system about printing devices you can access and where they are. Printing devices are typically given a proper name to make them easier to remember. Ask your system administrator for the names of the printing devices that you have access to. There will also be a printer environment variable set in your *.login* file located under your home directory. (This is covered under the chapter on home directories.) This set specifies the name of the primary printing device you will usually use. This way you will not have to specify the name of the printer each time you use it.

If your system administrator has done his or her job correctly, printing should be as easy as the command shown above.

If you wanted to print the file to a printer other than the one you normally print to, there is an option to the "**lpr**" command that will enable you to specify alternate printing devices. This option is the -P option. Here is the command to send the same *phonelist* file to another printer:

ltahoe% **lpr -P(printername) phonelist**

(Remember, you must have other printers defined in your */etc/ printcap* file for this option to work.)

12-2 Printing Multiple Copies

If you wish to print more than one copy of your phonelist file, you may specify this in the command line:

ltahoe% **lpr -#3 phonelist**

12-3 Checking the Print Queue with the "lpq" Command

When you send a print job to a printing device, the system which is driving the printer (sometimes called a print server) places the job in a spooler. The spooler is a directory which contains all of the print jobs that are waiting to be printed. This is usually referred to as the print queue. The spooler's function is to prevent more than one print job from attempting to print at the same time. The term "spool" is derived from "Simultaneous Peripheral Output On-Line".

The lpq command is used to check where your job is in the queue. If you are checking the queue of your default printer, the command would be:

ltahoe% **lpq**

The output you would receive would look like this:

```
ltahoe% lpq
(printername) is ready and printing

Rank       Owner       Job    Files         Total Size
active     bugs        902    myle          1807548 bytes
1st        tweetie     971    standard          762 bytes
                              input
2nd        sylvester   975    junk              988 bytes
3rd        speedy      177    standard          858 bytes
                              input
4th        miker       544    phonelist         767 bytes
```

The output shows that the user bugs is currently printing a job and tweetie is next in line. You can also see that bugs is printing a large file by the number of bytes in the file. The phonelist file is fourth on the list.

You can also use the menu option in SunView to check the printer queue. The chapter on SunView will explain how to select the print queue option from the menu.

12-4 Removing a Print Job from the Queue with **lprm**

If you sent a job to the printer, and then changed your mind about printing it, you can remove the job from the print queue with the "**lprm**" command.

To use this command you must first obtain the "job number" from the **lpq** output. If you look in the example above, the phonelist job number is 544. To remove this job from the queue, enter the command:

```
ltahoe% lprm 544
```

The system will then dequeue the print job from the spooler. You must be the owner of the job in order to remove it from the queue. This prevents rushed users from removing all the jobs in the queue so they can print their own jobs.

Note: You cannot use **lprm** on an active job. Once the job is printing, you cannot remove it.

There are many options to the **lpr** command that are covered in the Sun Commands Reference Manual. Preview them to see what else is available.

System Security

13

13-1 Security for the User

When using your Sun system, there will come a time either now or later when you will want to be sure there are no unauthorized users getting into your system and possibly getting at information that is private or confidential.

The best way to remove this fear is to make your system as secure as you can before the need arises. Keeping a secure system is not only a good practice but may save you some grief later on down the road.

It is said that "no system is completely secure". This may be true, but from a users' standpoint, you can make illegal entry as difficult as possible. This is accomplished in several ways. You will start by seeing some of the precautions that you as a user can do. You will learn each in detail.

1) Use special passwords

2) Set correct permissions on files and directories

3) Use file encryption

4) Restrict other user's capabilities

5) Use lockscreens

6) Cautions on superuser

13-2 Special Passwords

As you learned earlier in Chapter 1 on logging into your system, you should change your password as soon as you log on for the first time. This is done with the passwd command. (We explained this command earlier.) One of the best security measures in UNIX is to have a password that is difficult for someone to decipher. Passwords are stored in the file /etc/passwd. They are encrypted so that nobody can read your password. It is possible for someone to "guess" your password if you choose words like a person's name, abcd, standard words from the dictionary, etc. When choosing a password you should use non-standard words that contain capital letters or numbers. Misspelled words are good too. An example of some difficult passwords to break are:

time2go   my__sistem   let'swerk   Go4it   Sun__Tan

Your choice should be at least six characters long, and contain characters like the ones described above. You should never write your password down. If it is too difficult to remember, change it to something you can. Never use the same password on more than one system. Although your yp password should be the same as your regular system password, you should not have the same password for accounts on different workstations. Most important, change your password regularly. At least once every three to four months is a good plan.

The same rules apply to your root or superuser password as well. If you are allowed root access to your system, you must take extra care when becoming root. Never leave a system logged in as root, the root symbol (#) is a flag to someone who may not be honest.

13-3 Permissions on Your Home Directory

Once you have your home directory established, you will want to ensure that nobody can log into your system and browse through your files. You can protect yourself from this by setting the correct file permissions from the start. If you read Chapter 3 on permissions, you now understand how they work. You should check to see what the permissions are on your home directory. You will not want anyone else to be able to read your files or possibly write or delete files from your system. To do this check the current settings. Here is an example of poor permissions on a user's directory:

drwxrwsrwx 15 miker 2560 Dec 30 07:57 /home/ltahoe/miker

Notice that anyone can read the files, write to the directory, or remove anything they wish. A more secure permission setting would be:

drwx------ 15 miker 2560 Dec 30 10:37 /home/ltahoe/miker

Now only miker can read or write to the directory. If you will need other users to look at files in your home directory, you can add the read permission for your group. If you need your group to have read permission but do not want them to be able to read certain files, you can encrypt the files you want protected.

Be sure your umask is set to 022 for no write access by anyone, 002 if you want your group to have write access. Go back to the section on Permissions if you don't know about the umask.

13-4 File Encryption

There is a command called "**crypt**" which will take a file and turn it into a complete mess through file encryption, which only you can read by supplying the crypt command with a passwd for the file. In other words, **crypt** will take a file and alter it so that it is unreadable. Only the file password will allow you to read or edit the file again. The syntax for crypt is: crypt (password) < filename > filename.crypt The "<" and ">" are redirects. In English the command would read: crypt password, take input from file, create new file. Here is an example of how crypt works.

```
ltahoe% more slogan
Now is the time for all good men to come to
the aid---
ltahoe% crypt mypasswd  < slogan >  slogan.crypt
```

You would now have two files, the original *slogan* file, and a new file called *slogan.crypt*. If you try to look at the file *slogan.crypt,* you would see a bunch of garbage.

```
ltahoe% more slogan.crypt
M 2qdoac*d.E^ty# ;{*E
```

Be sure to remove the readable file after you have created the encrypted file. To look at the encrypted file, just use crypt command with the password:

```
ltahoe% crypt (mypasswd)  < slogan.crypt >  slogan
```

If you do not give the password to the crypt command, it will ask you for one.

```
ltahoe% crypt < slogan.crypt
Enter key:
```

Try to create a few files and encrypt them. Be sure to remember the password for each file. Once you forget, the file is as good as gone.

You can also vi encrypted files with the -x option. You must have the password in order to vi the file.

```
1tahoe% vi -x slogan.crypt
Enter le encryption key:
```

Once you enter the key, you can edit the readable file.

Read the man page on crypt for more information.

13-5 Restriction of Other Users

If your Sun system is in a networked environment, then chances are you can all log into each others' systems. This can present a problem in that you need to know what others are allowed to do on "your" system. There are several steps you can take to restrict access from other users' systems. If your company is running the yellow pages database, any user in the password file may log into your system unless you remove the "+" sign at the end of the file. The + allows anyone in the password database to log into your system. Check with your system administrator to arrange for restricted logins if you feel you need them. You can substitute the + sign for a list of users whom you need to have access.

13-6 Hosts.equiv File

There is a file in */etc* called *hosts.equiv*. This file contains a list of trusted systems and users. The format of the file is: hostname [username]

If there is a + sign in the file, any system that your machine knows about can have access. This file can be important if you only want a few systems and users to be able to access your system. You can also deny access to specific groups with a -@group. Read the man page for hosts.equiv. You will find it valuable reading.

13-7 Users .rhosts File

You can create a file in your home directory called .rhosts. This file has the same format as the *hosts.equiv* file. Here you can give or deny access for the specific user attempting to log in. Where the *hosts.equiv* file will allow any user logging in from a specified host access, the *.rhosts* file will only allow access from a host to the user in the *.rhosts* file in your home directory. Since this file is read before the *hosts.equiv* file, if you deny access to someone in *hosts.equiv*, they would gain access if they were in the *.rhosts* file.

13-8 Lockscreens

If you are going to be leaving your system unattended for a while, you should either log off of the system, or bring up a lockscreen. The lockscreen is a random pattern that covers up your screen. The lockscreen can only be removed if you enter your password. Leaving a system open is an invitation for someone to gain access. The lockscreen command can be found in the SunView rootmenu. By holding down the right mouse button in a grey area of the screen, there will be a selection called lockscreen. If you select it, the lockscreen program will begin and your window environment will stay intact behind the screen program. To get back to your window environment, simply hit any key and the lockscreen will stop and ask you for your password. Enter your password and Sunview will re-appear as you left it.

13-9 Caution on Superuser Access
Root .rhosts File

Like the users' *.rhosts* file, there is a file under / called *.rhosts*. Hosts listed in this file may log into your system as superuser and will not be prompted for a password. This is very dangerous and unless you have a specific reason for allowing this you should not have any entries in this file. If someone wanted to track down the other system, they may be able to gain superuser access and then get onto your system. If you need to give someone /.rhosts access, be sure it is only temporary and remove it as soon as you are finished.

Rebooting Your System

14

14-1 Reboot Methods

There may be occasions where you may need to reboot your system. A program may lock the system or a process may have quit that can only be restarted by a system reboot.

There are several ways to reboot your system. Here is a list of reboot procedures. Some methods will depend on the status of the system and whether or not you have keyboard access.

The following commands will perform a reboot (all of these commands require root access):

reboot	This will reboot the system and perform disk checks with fsck.
halt	This will halt the system and return it to the monitor prompt ">". Upon reboot, the system will perform disk checks with fsck.
fasthalt	This will halt the system to the monitor prompt ">". Upon reboot, the system will not perform disk checks.
L1A	This will abort the system to the monitor prompt ">". This is a last resort method of rebooting the system.

You will start by learning which method is best for a given situation. The main reason for bringing down the system gracefully is to keep from corrupting your disks. When the system is running, the disks are open for writes. If the system is aborted without closing the disks, you may encounter some file corruption. When you execute correct rebooting procedures, the system will close the disks prior to rebooting or halting the system. This process is referred to as "syncing the disks". There is a command called **sync**, which performs this task. Before rebooting, you should run the **sync** command at least twice, just to be sure.

```
ltahoe# sync
ltahoe# sync
```

The **reboot, halt** and **fasthalt** commands will perform the syncing operation automatically. Most users run the **sync** command as a precaution anyway.

14-2 Reboot

The reboot command is entered on the command line. You must be root in order to execute the reboot command.

ltahoe# **reboot**

The system will sync the disks and perform a system reboot automatically. When booting, the system will perform full disk checks on all file systems which are specified in the */etc/fstab* file. This is the most preferred method of rebooting your system.

14-3 Halt

The **halt** command is entered on the command line and must be run as root. This command will sync the disks, halt your system, and place you at the monitor prompt.

ltahoe# **halt**

To boot your system, from the monitor prompt, enter "**b**" (for boot).

>**b**

When the system boots, a full file system check will be performed.

14-4 Fasthalt

This command will perform the same task as halt will, with the exception of performing disk checks when booting. This command is usually run by the system administrator when a server or other critical system needs to be rebooted, but cannot be down for the length of time needed for a full file system check. The administrator can run the disk checks later once the system is back on line. (You must be root to run this command.)

ltahoe# **fasthalt**

To boot the system from the monitor prompt, enter "**b**" (for boot).

>**b**

14-5 L1A

This sequence of keys, the "**L1**" key and the "**a**" key depressed in sequence, will abort the system to the monitor prompt without syncing the disks. This method should only be used when you have no keyboard control of any kind. The procedure for aborting the system is to hold down the L1 key (that's the key in the upper left hand corner of the keyboard), and then depress the "a" key. You may encounter file system corruptions when you boot the system. The fsck program will check the disks and should be able to correct any errors. You do not have to be root to execute this key sequence.

Check with your system administrator before you do this because he or she may be able to log in from another system and halt the system gracefully for you.

Note: If you perform the L1A sequence by mistake, you can get back into the UNIX environment by entering a "c" for continue. This will work provided you have not entered any other keys after **L1A** sequence.

Future Reading

After reading this book you will have the basic understanding of how to use your Sun workstation. You should continue reading the Sun Guides which came with your system to further develop you skills on the system. The Sun guides will go into greater detail regarding specific functions to the applications.

The man pages will prove invaluable to you when you begin to experiment with new commands. The man pages are easily accessible and will save you vast amounts of access time rather than trying to flip through the encyclopedia size documentation package.

If you are trying to enhance your UNIX skills, you should take a look at the following list of books. They have much to offer regarding the basic understanding of UNIX.

Rachel Morgan, Henry McGilton,
Introducing UNIX System V,
McGraw-Hill,
1987

Kathy Slattery, George Becker
System Administrators Guide to the Sun Workstation,
Springer-Verlag,
1990

Rachel Morgan, Henry McGilton,
Introducing the UNIX System,
McGraw-Hill,
1983

Index

ypmatch command, 159–160
yppasswd command, 160
ypserv daemon, 159
ypwhich command, 160

Zero level dump, 173

-9 signal, 40

> character, 41
: command, 55
/ command, 55–56
? command, 56
+ sign, 37, 151, 188
− sign, 37

sign, 84
/ symbol, 10
% symbol, 36–37
& symbol, 38
! symbol, 45, 153
$ symbol, 45–46
$^\wedge$ symbol, 46
\ symbol, 84
> symbol, 87
@ symbol, 149
* symbol, 177
| symbol, 43
" " symbols, 43
( ) symbols, 86
< > symbols, 125